25 Years of Space Photography

Jet Propulsion Laboratory

California Institute of Technology

This exhibition is made possible by a grant from the IBM Corporation.

The Baxter Art Gallery exhibition program is made possible by a grant from the Pasadena Art Alliance.

Cover: IRAS photo mosaic of the center of our galaxy. 1983. False color.

25 Years of Space Photography

Jet Propulsion Laboratory

California Institute of Technology

Published by the Baxter Art Gallery, California Institute of Technology, Pasadena, California,

in association with W. W. Norton & Company, New York and London

The photographs in this exhibition were made by the Jet Propulsion Laboratory for NASA.

This book is dedicated, with respect and affection, to David R. Smith,

founding Director and Chairman of the Board of Governors of the Baxter Art Gallery.

Baxter Art Gallery
May 22 — July 31, 1985

IBM Gallery of Science and Art
November 5, 1985 — January 4, 1986

David M. Grether, *Chairman*
Division of the Humanities and
Social Sciences,
California Institute of Technology

Jay Belloli, *Director*, Baxter Art
Gallery

Barbara Alexander, *Assistant to
the Director and Registrar*

Brian Forrest, *Preparator*

Edited by Andrea P. A. Belloli and
Lynne Dean

Designed in Los Angeles by
Jeffrey Mueller

Typography by Type Works,
Pasadena, California

Lithography by The Castle Press,
Pasadena, California

Copyright © 1985 by the Baxter
Art Gallery,
California Institute of Technology,
Pasadena, California 91125

All rights reserved

W. W. Norton & Company, Inc.,
500 Fifth Avenue,
New York, New York 10110

W. W. Norton & Company Ltd,
37 Great Russell Street,
London WC1B 3NU

Published simultaneously in
Canada by Penguin Books
Canada Ltd, 2801 John Street,
Markham, Ontario L3R 1B4

Library of Congress Catalog No.
85-071321

ISBN 0-393-02280-3 (cloth)
ISBN 0-393-30291-1 (paper)

Table of Contents

6 Foreword

6 Preface and Acknowledgments

8 The Persistent Observer

20 Catalogue

Ranger 22

Surveyor 26

Lunar Orbiter 32

Mariner 4,6,7 36

Mariner 9 42

Mariner 10 48

Viking 54

Voyager / Jupiter 66

Voyager / Saturn 78

Seasat 88

IRAS 94

SIR-A and SIR-B 102

Galileo 111

112 Chronology of Missions

116 Appendix

For the last quarter of a century, Caltech's Jet Propulsion Laboratory has been a major participant in the United States' program of space exploration for scientific purposes. This program has included missions to the Moon, observations of the Earth from space, and astronomical observations from an orbiting telescope. The most dramatic missions have been a series of voyages to all of the planets of our solar system as far as Saturn; a spacecraft is now en route to Uranus and Neptune.

The spacecraft which have performed these missions are complex laboratories containing a number of instruments designed to obtain various scientific data. Some of the most important data have been the images returned from space. In preparing this exhibition, "25 Years of Space Photography: Jet Propulsion Laboratory, California Institute of Technology," many of the best images returned by JPL flight projects have been collected. With one exception, Lunar Orbiter, none of these images were obtained with a camera and photographic film; most were created by means of a special form of television camera, using a set of filters for color information. Some images are from radar observations. The Infrared Astronomical Satellite (IRAS) did not form images in the usual sense but was a scanning telescope which generated an electrical signal when a star passed a narrow opening in the focal plane.

All of the images illustrated here were transmitted from space and reassembled on Earth using computers. This processing of the images on Earth has become a technique in which JPL is unusually competent. The data is corrected for errors and adjusted in perspective and scale; many different images are combined to present a single one with color, intensity and detail most useful to the scientific analyst. The results are pictures of extraordinary scientific value to specialists. Coincidentally these images have provided a means by which to communicate mission results to non-specialists with clarity and impact.

Many of these pictures are unquestionably beautiful. They present a panorama of regions few of us are likely to visit and one that the human eye could not, by itself, record. The electronic processing which was done to enhance interpretabilty was performed by experts who also had an eye for beauty. I believe these are works of art. They inform, inspire, and evoke thoughts of worlds unseen.

Dr. Lew Allen
Director
Jet Propulsion Laboratory

The complex, enigmatic, and astonishing images assembled in this volume speak of the parallels between art and science in ways that are unexpected. Originally created for reasons of scientific research, these photographs, with their expressive color, unusual spatial qualities, and exceptional contrasts of light and dark, have functioned as unprecedented aids in the study of celestial bodies. Often, as might be expected, these images have raised more scientific questions than they have answered. Unexpectedly, perhaps, they have raised artistic questions as well. In fact the very combination of inspiration, experimentation, and hard work that brought them into being has obvious parallels with the early modern conception of the artistic process. This conception has in common with the scientific method an emphasis on intuition on the one hand and logic on the other; the term "beautiful" is often used in speaking of the somehow satifying and appropriate end-product of both — whether a painting or a mathematical equation.

Marcel Duchamp's meditations on the necessity of involving both artist and viewer in determining what constitutes a work of art unavoidably come to mind as one looks at these images. While they are, in a sense, "found objects," their aesthetic qualities are underscored by their being included in this book and in the exhibition it accompanies; though their primary function — indeed, their reason for existing at all — has nothing whatever to do with Art, their aesthetic power and significance, while difficult to articulate, are undeniable.

But the issues, it turns out, are even more

complex. For one accustomed to thinking of art and science as mutually exclusive categories, it is surprising to discover that these photographs often were created by means of series of undeniably artistic decisions. Colors, for example, were enhanced to make given images more pleasing to the eye. The selection of images to include in a Martian photomosaic or of the hues for the jewel-like SIR-B image of the Island of Hawaii turn out to have been arbitrary and — in many ways — purely aesthetic. At times decisions were made simply to see "what would happen if . . ." — if an image was manipulated — "stretched," beefed up, toned down.

Finally, these images — and the endeavors of both art and science — are about human need: the need to know, to find answers, to create. In this sense, although none of the images included in "25 Years of Space Photography" was taken by a single human being with camera in hand, and although no human figures inhabit their landscapes, these strange, alien, but somehow knowable pictures ultimately speak of our humanity.

•

Assembling this exhibition has been an extremely complex undertaking involving the talents and efforts of a large number of organizations and individuals. At Caltech, David R. Smith initially put me in touch with Dr. Albert R. Hibbs, one of the individuals most responsible for the development of JPL's space program. Dr. Hibbs introduced me in turn to Frank Colella and Jurrie van der Woude, also at JPL; this exhibition would have been inconceivable without Mr. van der Woude's involvement, knowledge, and tireless

assistance. Dr. Lew Allen, Director, JPL, is to be thanked for his encouragement and his willingness to write the foreword to this book. The JPL Public Information Office, which, in effect, allowed me to move in on a part-time basis, has been wonderfully helpful, particularly Don Bane, Yolanda Blevin, Frank Bristow, Henry Fuhrmann, Alison Galien, Mary Beth Murrill, Yvonne Samuel, and Alan Wood. Along with Dr. Hibbs, Don Lynn and Cathy LeVine, also of JPL, generously allowed their comments and observations to be included in this catalogue. Terre Ashmore-Davis, Mary Di Salvo, Ben Holt, Gina Nelson, Bob Post, Joe Stockemer, and many others at JPL who provided assistance have my gratitude.

At Caltech, David Grether has been continuously encouraging and helpful. I am grateful for Caltech's permission to apply to the IBM Corporation to fund this exhibition and publication. Barbara Alexander, Baxter Art Gallery, has worked long hours on many aspects of the exhibition, and I deeply appreciate her help. Gail Peterson deserves sincere thanks as well, as do Phyllis Brewster, Susan Davis, Jane Dietrich, Kathy Harris, Tanya Mink, Brian Forrest, Curtis Berak, and Stephen Berens.

This book could not have been created without the unequaled assistance of Andrea P. A. Belloli, who served as coordinating editor. Lynne Dean provided invaluable editorial support. Christopher Knight is to be commended for his superb essay, written under outrageous time constraints. Jeffrey Mueller provided the elegant design for this book and the exhibition poster; Don Morgan, Type Works, and The Castle Press,

Pasadena, realized Mr. Mueller's conceptions. Typecraft, Pasadena, printed the exhibition brochure and invitation, also designed by Mr. Mueller. W. W. Norton and Company, New York and London, have generously agreed to distribute this volume, and I would like to thank them for their assistance, particularly James Mairs.

This exhibition could not have occurred without the support of the IBM Corporation. I am deeply grateful for their generosity and interest. I am also profoundly appreciative of the interest and support of the Pasadena Art Alliance, which for eight years has made the Baxter Art Gallery's exhibition program possible. Finally I want to express my respect and gratitude to JPL as an institution. Without the efforts of thousands of individuals at that facility over the last twenty-five years, the extraordinary images included here simply would not exist. I am happy to be able to thank Caltech for its fifteen years of support of the Baxter Art Gallery by honoring the Jet Propulsion Laboratory through this, the gallery's closing exhibition.

Jay Belloli
Director
Baxter Art Gallery

Early in the fall of 1846, U. J. J. Leverrier, a young French mathematician, sent a letter to Johann Gottfried Galle, an assistant at the Berlin Observatory. Intrigued by mathematical calculations that suggested the existence of a planet beyond Uranus, which had been located just sixty-five years earlier, Leverrier sought assistance from the astronomer in verifying these calculations. "I would like to find a persistent observer," he wrote to Galle,

> who would be willing to devote some time to an examination of a part of the sky in which there may be a planet to discover. . . . I demonstrate that it is impossible to satisfy the observations of Uranus without introducing the action of a new planet, thus far unknown; and remarkably, there is only one single position in the ecliptic where this perturbing planet can be located.

Galle received Leverrier's letter on September 23. Two days later, he excitedly replied to his colleague in France:

> The planet whose position you have pointed out *actually exists*. The same day that I received your letter, I found a star of the eighth magnitude. . . . The observations made the following day determined this was the sought-for planet.[1]

This, the eighth satellite of the Sun, came to be called Neptune.

Eventually, further dogged examination revealed that Neptune itself was subject to perturbations caused by yet another unknown cosmic body. As with Uranus before it, the chronicling of irregularities in the eighth planet's motion was to lead to speculation concerning the probable existence of a trans-Neptunian planet. Clyde W. Tombaugh, an American farmer and amateur astronomer, discovered Pluto in 1930. At the Lowell Observatory, using a telescope fitted with a camera, Tombaugh exposed photographic plates at two-day intervals. Between the first exposure and the second, he noted a small but nonetheless distinct shift in a spot of light of the fifteenth magnitude: the existence of a trans-Neptunian planet, some 3.7 billion miles from the Sun, had been verified.

Between the exposure of Neptune, in 1846, and the exposure of Pluto, in 1930, Leverrier's plea for a "persistent observer" capable of devoting time to a steady and unyielding examination of "a part of the sky" had been answered — and in a revolutionary way. Born, ironically, less than twenty years before the Frenchman deposited his letter to his German colleague in the post, the camera — a robotic form whose existence Leverrier doubtless had not anticipated — was to become that persistent observer in the exploration of space. A century and a half later, having photographed the Moon and the planets from Mercury through Saturn, cameras aboard spacecraft are about to photograph those perturbed planets, Uranus and Neptune.

•

I am looking at a color photograph of the surface of Mars (*fig. 1*). An explanatory caption accompanying it explains:

> This is the first color photograph taken by Viking Lander 2 and shows a rocky and reddish surface very much like that photographed by Lander 1 more than 4000 miles away. The camera is facing approximately northeast. The photograph was taken in the late afternoon, and the Sun is behind the camera. Because the spacecraft is tilted about 8 degrees toward the west, the horizon appears tilted. In fact, the horizon is nearly level.[2]

Certain words and phrases in this concise, descriptive text dislodge themselves from the rest: "the first"; "very much like"; "approximately northeast"; "the late afternoon"; "behind the camera"; "8 degrees"; "the west"; "appears"; "in fact." Most of these are terms that attempt to identify location, in space and in time, words that suggest a complex system of coordinates which acknowledges the interrelationships among compass points, relative placement, comparative space, general quality of light, sequence, and time.

The first unit of photographic information transmitted by Viking Lander 2 to Earth from the oxidized surface of Mars is located in the upper left corner of the photograph, in the topmost register. It is a minuscule square of visual data — called a pixel — of pale orange hue. The video camera aboard the landing craft scanned the vista in sequential bits — from left to right, from top to bottom — assigning to each a number between one and 255 on a gray scale. The hundreds of thousands of pixels were gathered during a time span of approximately ninety seconds' duration. Together these accumulated pixels are rather like sequential frames in a film, or the words printed across the surface of this page. To read the pixels in the order of their creation and reception is to read

1. Morton Grosser, *The Discovery of Neptune* (Cambridge, Mass., 1962), pp. 115-116.

2. Jet Propulsion Laboratory, California Institute of Technology, *Viking: The Exploration of Mars* (Pasadena, 1974), p. 42.

Figure 1.
The first Viking Lander 2 color
photograph of the surface of
Mars. 9/76 (EC).

the history of that flat landscape we call a photograph.

As for the depicted landscape of Mars, it's desolate, a rock-strewn desert opening wide beneath a flat and sulfurous sky whose color drains toward gray. Thin veils of dust shroud the foreground rocks, whose dispersion in the camera's field of vision is random and seemingly inarticulate. The light is harsh, the shadows sharp. The vast depth of this barren field, which begins with visible grains of stone and continues to a far and unfocused horizon, is held in tension by the flat grid of pixels anchored to the picture's surface. Between the moment when the video camera inaugurated its scan at the upper left and the moment it completed its methodical journey at the lower right, what happened on the surface of Mars? Did one small pebble, or even an ounce of dust, shift its position in an imperceptible breeze? What features existed beyond this photographic field? Cropped as it is on all four sides, what lay to the right and to the left? Did the "level" horizon mentioned in the explanatory caption explode into a mountain range or sink into an ancient crater?

The Viking Lander 2 camera did not merely frame a landscape on Mars, nor did it only frame answers to scientific speculations on the nature of that terrestrial planet. The camera framed questions, too, questions about the world lying beyond this particular image. That the frame so clearly *excludes* compels us to imagine beyond its limits. Like each pixel in the sequence that constitutes the unified picture, this specific image is itself a fragmentary utterance in the unified image of the planet. What this barren image has

to say is only fully spoken *in relation to* the next photograph sent back to Earth — and the next, and the next, and, finally, to all that were received. To read the tens of thousands of pictures sent back from Mars, beginning with the twenty-one vague photographs from the 1965 flyby spacecraft, Mariner 4, and ending with the last of the thousands transmitted before the final Viking Lander ceased operation in November 1982, is not simply to read a history of the planet. It is to participate in the making of that history. In space, as on Earth, the camera appears to be a tool of mere transcription; in fact, it plays a role in making the world that it depicts as image. Space photography is an instrument of construction.

•

Paradoxically, the more we have come to know of our natural habitat, the deeper we have gotten into the wilderness. In fact, one could even say that the increase in humankind's knowledge of nature made the invention of the eighteenth-century idea of wilderness necessary. To conceive of nature as the touchstone or the norm was, after all, to establish a criterion for goodness and morality, both of the individual and of society, a criterion whose existence intrinsically cultivated and inhabited any "natural" region with the presence of human thought. The British poet Alexander Pope, equating knowledge of nature with the then-new science of astronomy, wrote in his "Essay on Man" (1734) that the *truly* natural human being had to shed the vanity of such knowledge, for — in Pope's estimation — the untutored mind

Sees God in clouds, or hears him in the

wind;
His soul proud Science never taught to stray
Far as the solar walk or milky way;
Yet simple nature to his hope has giv'n,
Behind the cloud-topped hill, an humbler
    Heav'n. . . .[3]

For Pope, nature was a divinely ordered system of relationships. Art, on the other hand, was any intellectually ordered system, including "proud Science." In order to retrieve nature, then, all conscious and deliberate alterations in the raw material of experience had to be jettisoned. For if one knew "naturally," to prefer art to nature was to create a wilderness.

The constructed imagery of nature called landscape painting is a relatively recent phenomenon in the history of Western art. Isolated examples can be found as early as 1338 in Italy (Ambrogio Lorenzetti's allegorical fresco for Siena's Palazzo Pubblico), and later easel paintings by Giorgione, Claude, Gainsborough, Watteau, and several Dutch artists are familiar. Yet even in these, the landscape is populated by shepherds, nymphs, peasants, or finely clothed aristocrats. It is nature known, or at least nature depicted in relation to man's presence or actions; for Lorenzetti, indeed, the undulating hills have been made subservient to the social constructions of the city. Landscape paintings without figures, which thus evoke the idea that nature in itself is a potential source of meaning, did not come into their own until the 1800s. The idea is thus a modern one. In Church's painting of the roaring torrent of Niagara Falls surrounded by tiny dwellings, or in Monet's many pictures of grainstacks (*figs. 2 and 3*), the natural site is a

3. Alexander Pope, "Essay on Man," in Charles M. Coffin, ed., *The Major Poets: English and American* (New York, 1954), p. 240.

place where man's authority, at the very least, is incomplete.

This normative use of nature, which equates the natural with the good or the omnipotent, attempted a reconciliation between the idea of perfect order and regularity in the physical world and the self-evident corruption and chaos of human life. Astrology, the divination of influences dictated from space, had provided an earlier model for understanding these conflicting states, by inventing a superlunary world of ordered regularity and a sublunary world of pandemonium and turmoil. Thus, there were thought to be two natures, the first of which, a powerful force, acted on the second, a passive object: Nature "beyond the moon" created and was uncreated; nature "below" was created and uncreating.

The classic ascent to the perfect world of uncorrupted order, of course, historically has taken the paths of mysticism and of religion. In the secular terms of the eighteenth century, this world also could be reached by way of imagination. Joseph Addison, whose *The Pleasures of the Imagination* (1712) codified many of the basic tenets of the idea of the Sublime for the early 1700s, revealed the profound impact of the new telescopic (and microscopic) worlds of nature on that of philosophy. For Addison, "a spacious horizon" was "an image of liberty."[4] His dazzling picture of perfect freedom encouraged later writers to "travel" to the stars. For example, Lorenzo, the protagonist in Edward Young's *Night Thoughts* (1745-46), embarked upon a sublime and cosmic voyage to the enlarging space of infinity newly

Figure 2.
Frederic Edwin Church.
American, 1826-1900. **Niagara Falls**, *1857. Oil on canvas. 42½ × 90½". The Corcoran Gallery of Art, Washington, D.C. Museum Purchase.*

Figure 3.
Claude Monet. French, 1840-1926. **The Grainstack**, *1891. Oil on canvas. 25⁹⁄₁₆ × 36³⁄₁₆". The Art Institute of Chicago. Mr. and Mrs. Daniel C. Searle restricted gift; Major Acquisitions Centennial Fund.*

4. Joseph Addison, *The Spectator,* ed. Donald E. Bond (Oxford, 1965), p. 189.

pictured through the telescope:

How great,

How glorious, then, appears the mind of
man

When in it all the stars, and planets, roll![5]

As a creation of the mind, the wilderness was a
place to be visited in the imagination.

•

Photographic imagery made in space was
the subject of an exhibition mounted in 1981 by
the Grey Art Gallery at New York University.
Among much else, the catalogue accompanying
"The Photography of Space Exploration"
correctly pointed out that conducting
photographic expeditions to locate and chart the
geographical and geological features encountered
at the frontiers — the wilderness — is a
tradition whose birth followed closely on the
heels of the invention of the medium itself, first
with daguerreotypes and then with wet-plates,
hand-held and electronic cameras, and — now
— by means of computer-generated photographs
collected from deep space.[6] As is well known, J.
M. Stanley, who photographically charted the
wilds of Missouri while on an 1853 survey
empowered by Congress, was followed in later
decades by William Henry Jackson, Timothy
O'Sullivan, Eadweard Muybridge, Carleton
Watkins, and others. The first photograph taken
from the wilderness of space was made just five
years after Stanley's survey, in 1858, when
Gaspard-Félix Tournachon — known as Nadar —
made a collodion positive, no longer extant, from
a balloon in which he had ascended above the
village of Petit Bicêtre, just outside Paris
(fig. 4). Like the Seasat photographs in this

NADAR. élevant la Photographie à la hauteur de l'Art

Figure 4.
Honoré Daumier. French,
1808-1879. **Nadar elevating**
Photography to the level of Art,
1862. Lithograph. International
Museum of Photography at
George Eastman House.

Figure 5.
Seasat radar image of the area
near Ames, Iowa, with the pattern
of fields clearly visible. Darker
areas are where rain had recently
fallen. 8/16/78 (B/W).

5. H. J. Pettit, *A Bibliography of
Edward Young's Night Thoughts*
(Boulder, 1954), p. 279.

6. Robert Littman, ed., *The
Photography of Space
Exploration* (New York, 1981), p.
5.

exhibition, Nadar's frontier or wilderness was not merely an unmapped place newly depicted, but an uncharted point of view newly experienced *(fig. 5)*. Timothy O'Sullivan, who had distinguished himself as a member of Mathew Brady's photographic corps during the Civil War, joined the first of Clarence King's United States Geological Explorations of the Fortieth Parallel in 1867. The twenty-seven-year-old photographer's job, common to his new profession in general, was twofold: first, to function as a scientific technician, recording the landscape in a documentary manner, and second, to act as a publicist, making photographs whose significance would encourage further expeditions. In 1978, when photographer Rick Dingus retraced O'Sullivan's steps in order to rephotograph the same sites more than a century later to discover if, and how, they had changed, he made a startling discovery. A remarkable difference between Dingus' and O'Sullivan's photographs of a stack of boulders in Weber Valley, Utah, is that, in one, the horizon is nearly level, while in the other, it is a gentle slope *(figs. 6 and 7)*. O'Sullivan's photograph was made with a tripod and camera pitched nine degrees from the horizontal. Not unlike the Viking Lander 2's color photograph of the Martian landscape *(fig. 1)*, this nineteenth-century documentary photograph of the wilderness contains an artificial horizon.

Rarely, if ever, does a photograph contain its own documentation. Its status as a document is external to itself (hence the explanatory caption describing interrelated coordinates in the image of Mars photographed by Viking Lander 2, or the revelatory comparison between the two

Figure 6.
Timothy O'Sullivan. American, ca. 1840-1882. **Tertiary Conglomerates, Weber Valley, Utah,** *ca. 1868. Albumen print from a glass negative. Approx. 9 × 12". U.S. Geological Survey, Denver.*

Figure 7.
Rick Dingus. American, b. 1951. **Tertiary Conglomerates, Weber Valley (Witches Rocks #5),** *1978. Silver print. 9 × 12". ©Rick Dingus for the Rephotographic Survey Project, 1978.*

photographs of Weber Valley). That is, as Beaumont Newhall has observed, such status resides in the ways in which the photograph itself is documented or used. In the vivid images of Jupiter's Great Red Spot, photographed by Voyager 1 *(fig. 8)*, or in the IRAS photograph of the galactic center of the Milky Way (cover), where is "up," where is "down?" Looking at these photographs, where are *we*? We are standing on an artificial horizon. The unseen position of the spacecraft, its antennae locked into a trinity of coordinates consisting of the Sun and two stars like Columbus holding his ship steady on its navigational course, establishes our perceptual terra firma. Color, too, is imbedded in conditions of relativity external to the picture *(fig. 9)*. The turbulent cloud patterns to the left of the Great Red Spot are photographically reproduced as the human eye would see them aboard the hurtling spacecraft — or, in other photographs, they're split apart and peeled away through the use of photographic filters and computerized image-enhancement processes. In these pictures, false color is created in order to allow us to see more deeply than our eyes could see, to subsume our sight in the mechanically and electronically constructed vision of space. Thus, to look at these documentary photographs of the superlunary wilderness is to join Nadar in a newly experienced point of view, and to accompany O'Sullivan into the uncharted terrain of Weber Valley.

●

If the documentary status of a photograph is a matter of intent, on the part of the photographer, or of use, on the part of the viewer,

Figure 8.
A view from Voyager 1 of Jupiter's Great Red Spot, and beneath it, one of the planet's white ovals, both of which are anticyclonic vortices in the atmosphere. The Red Spot is two to three times the diameter of Earth. 3/79 (EC).

something unseen but ever-present assumes a position of prominence. As in photojournalism, documentary pictures offer evidence. News photographs say: "This is what the accused killer looks like"; "this is the scene where an undercover policeman busted teenage pushers at a suburban high school"; "these are the charred remains of the warehouse torched by an unknown arsonist." Yet news photographs have no such intrinsic meanings. Without benefit of caption or accompanying story they are empty images: the "accused killer" is but a picture of a scowling woman with shoulder-length hair and glasses; the "scene of the drug bust" is but a brick building on a tree-shaded street; the "target of the arsonist" is but a picture of an ashen ruin with smoke curling skyward. Alter the caption of the picture of a scowling woman to "victim of a mugging," and the evidence inextricably alters, too.

In the pages of this book, or framed and hanging on the walls of a gallery, space photographs are radically re-contextualized: they are transformed from offerings of visual evidence into aesthetic objects for examination. In this way, they are stripped of their malleable use as scientific, military, or political argument. The meaning of these images is emptied out. As a result, the focus begins to shift away from the relationship between the photographic image and its absent referent — the giant clouds of interstellar gas that dot the center of our galaxy, or the relative particle size of the various rings of Saturn. The focus shifts toward the relationship between the image and the photographer who made it.

Figure 9.
The same Voyager 1 photograph of Jupiter's Great Red Spot in false color to bring out finer detail in the cloud structure. A complex, dynamic cloud pattern develops in the Red Spot's wake. 3/79 (FC).

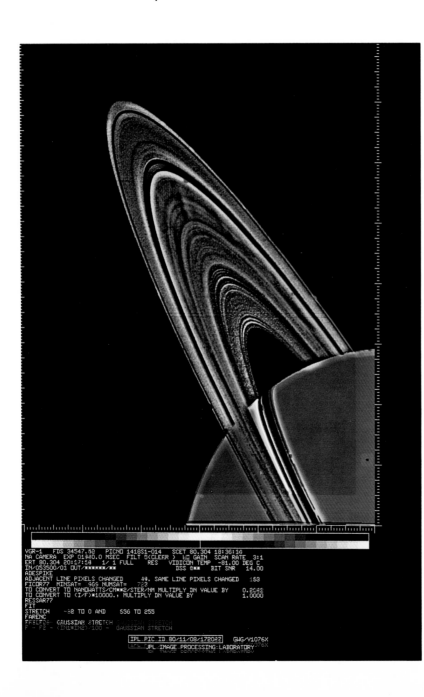

VGR-1   FDS 34547.62   PICNO 1418S1-014   SCET 80.304 18:36:16
NA CAMERA EXP 01940.0 MSEC   FILT 5(CLEER) LO GAIN   SCAN RATE   3:1
ERT 80.304 20:17:50   1/ 1 FULL   RES   VIDICON TEMP -81.00 DEG C
IN/053500/01 OUT/******/**   DSS ***   BIT SNR   14.00
ADESPIKE
ADJACENT LINE PIXELS CHANGED   49. SAME LINE PIXELS CHANGED   153
FICOR77 MINSAT= 966 NUMSAT=   722
TO CONVERT TO NANOWATTS/CM**2/STER/NM MULTIPLY DN VALUE BY   0.2048
TO CONVERT TO (I/F)*10000., MULTIPLY DN VALUE BY   1.0000
RESSAR77
FIT
STRETCH   -92 TO 0 AND   536 TO 255
FARENC
RFSLR2= GAUSSIAN STRETCH   GAUSSIAN STRETCH
F - F2 - (IN1*IN2)/100 - GAUSSIAN STRETCH

IPL PIC ID 80/11/08/172022   GWG/V1076X
JPL IMAGE PROCESSING LABORATORY

Figure 10.
Photograph of the rings of Saturn from Voyager 1, showing subtle color variations and previously unknown structural features. Spokes, ringlets, gaps, and waves are all visible in this photograph. 11/8/80 (FC).

Figure 11.
Photograph of Apollo 12 Astronaut Alan L. Bean on the Moon taken by Astronaut Charles Conrad, Jr. 11/19-20/69.

Who made these photographs? Who is the photographer? The single unifying feature of the numerous pictures illustrated in this book is that they were generated during unmanned missions in space. There was no Nadar sailing happily in a balloon, nor an O'Sullivan lugging heavy equipment across treacherous terrain, nor even a Charles Conrad, astronaut, standing on the lunar plains of Mare Procellarum with a camera strapped to his chest *(fig. 11)*. From these unmanned missions one will find no photographs of a human being's footprints in some extraterrestrial dust, only a picture of the cold, metallic footpad of Viking Lander 1 standing firmly on the Martian soil *(figs. 13 and 14)*.

The singular and independent photographer is here replaced by the diverse and interdependent multitude of scientists and technicians whose coordinated commands, responses, and actions set into motion a complex chain of events that results in a photographic image. Like the photographers who chronicled the unpopulated terrain of the American West at the end of the nineteenth century — explorers, adventurers, technicians — they are not artists. Yet if Timothy O'Sullivan and Carleton Watkins were without artistic ambitions in their image-making practices, the certifiable rarity of their vintage prints has nonetheless contributed to the fetishisation of their photographs as the products of fundamentally subjective vision — in other words, as works of Art. Space photographs are resistant to such individuated subjectivity. In keeping with their digital origination in a video camera, there is no material rarity involved, no unique original nor vintage print encoded with the subjective vision of the "artist's eye." This is far removed from the traditional notion of facture in painting — a notion that has been absorbed into the lexicon of photography-as-art — in which the visible evidence of the artist's manner of making becomes the identifying signature, the guarantor of authenticity and key to transcendent value. Rather, as Benjamin Buchloh has argued of Alexander Rodchenko's photographs from the late 1920s and 1930s,[7] space photographs venture a factographic claim: they seek to make reality visible without self-expressive interference or mediation. They are iconic representations of an absent referent, reveal the monumentality of the camera's awesome vision, and convey an undeniable sense of technological optimism *(fig. 12)*.

The viewfinder on a spacecraft's camera is conceptual, not visual. It's a dizzying array of mathematical calculations, worked out in advance and programmed into the robotic eye; conceptual vision lets us know just when it's time to "snap the shutter." Cartier-Bresson's "decisive moment" is here made wildly elastic, attenuated and twisted like a stretched rubber band, since an electronic signal sent from Earth to reprogram a spacecraft hurtling beyond Saturn will take hours to reach its destination. Today, on-board computers determine the percentage of available information-bits essential to the reception of the necessary data, thus composing the final picture within the conceptual viewfinder. Gravity, too, can contribute markedly to the final range of choices for the photographic subject: the path of Mariner 10 past Venus was chosen for gravitational reasons, because the pull of the planet on the passing spacecraft had to be calculated in such a way as to thrust Mariner onward in its trajectory toward Mercury, its ultimate destination. Mariner's flyby photographs of Venus thus record sights encountered along a prescribed interplanetary highway. In visual terms, though, the collective photographer was working blind, like the photojournalist who holds his camera high in the air in a calculated attempt (colored by a thousand variables) to capture a fleeting glimpse of a movie star over the heads of an adoring mob.

Yet, if the creation of these space photographs was transpersonal — that is, produced by the complex web of late twentieth-century technological culture — so, too, is their reception. The production of these images incorporates two essential features: they constitute a visual form determined by the needs of the spectator/patron, and they partake of the

Figure 12.
Alexander Rodchenko. Russian, 1891-1956. Chauffeur, 1933. Gelatin silver print. 11¼ × 16". The Museum of Modern Art. Mr. and Mrs. John Spencer Fund.

7. Benjamin H. D. Buchloh, "From Faktura to Factography," *October* (Fall 1984), pp. 83-118.

distribution network of communications media. In place of the unitary vintage print, there is a plurality of authentic copies. With a little patience, and a few dollars to cover costs, you can send away to the National Space Data Center in Maryland and receive an authentic copy of, say, Surveyor's photograph of a sunset on the moon. In this way, the pictures made on unmanned spaceflights are radically different from self-expressive views of natural wonders. They're more like superlunary postcards brought back from a trip to a Jovian "Grand Canyon" or to a "Glacier Park" on Saturn's moon, Enceladus. For the creation and reception of these photographs is synchronically collective. In this photographic chronicle of our voyages in space, we are both creator and actor in the narrative. Space photographs do indeed offer evidence, but it is simple proof that we, the collective operator of the camera, were there.

•

I am looking at a computer composite of four Voyager 1 photographs of a portion of Saturn and its famous rings *(fig. 10)*. It is a complicated picture, said in the accompanying explanatory caption to contain "a wealth of new information" on the planet and its orbiting dust. But I know nothing of planetary sciences, whose specialized language is necessary to read this picture's astronomical text. The image is

Figure 13.
Footprints on the Moon and leg of Apollo 11 Landing Module taken by Astronauts Neil A. Armstrong and Edwin E. Aldrin, Jr. 7/20/69.

Figure 14.
The first photograph taken on the surface of Mars (Viking Lander 1) 1/20/76 (B/W).

beautiful, with its wobbly chromatic range and indistinct contours, a product of the wizardry of computer-enhancement technology. (If Addison and his contemporaries were right in their distinctions, the smallness, smoothness, delicacy, and variation of space photographs make them Beautiful; it is the terror, obscurity, difficulty, and vastness of space itself that is Sublime.) Yet I tend to find thousands upon thousands of photographs, published for countless different reasons in the daily, weekly, and monthly press, to be beautiful as well. It's true that this image of Saturn has a particular curiosity value: there are three odd black dots on its surface, which the explanatory caption parenthetically refers to as "reseau marks, artifacts of Voyager camera system." But all cameras leave their own peculiar traces.

What gives this particular picture, and all those others taken on journeys in deep space, its freakish and incomparable quality of strangeness is not complicated. In fact it is daunting in its simplicity. This photograph repeats to me incessantly that *I will never see Saturn and its famous rings*. All photographs are historical, those illustrated here included; they're records of the meeting between a camera and a place, a person, a time that is in the past and irrecoverable. (This is why virtually any innocuous photograph becomes increasingly interesting the older that it gets.) What Roland Barthes called, in *Camera Lucida*, "that rather terrible thing that is there in every photograph: the return of the dead,"[8] is here in full view, insisting that I recognize my own mortality reflected in the picture. And yet, it's more than

that. For space photographs, perhaps alone among the endless pictures made since the first heliograph by the Frenchman Joseph-Nicephore Nièpce, do not bear testimony to the expectation that the camera's operator stood immediately on the opposite side of the lens from that historical place and time. To look at a photograph of Saturn and its famous rings is to look at an image whose absent referent no one has, or could ever have, seen.

Cameras traditionally record the past and the real. Space cameras invite the future, the desire to be in proximity to the subject, which will "someday" be realized. The emptiness of their constructed imagery is filled with the solicitations of science fiction. (It is appropriate that the very word "photograph" was proposed in 1839 to replace the pioneering Henry Fox Talbot's working phrase "photogenic drawing" by Sir John F. W. Herschel, the British astronomer.) The principle of the camera has been known for centuries, but not quite in this way. In the late Renaissance, the *camera obscura* (literally "dark room") came into common usage for the production of hand-drawn pictures that would subscribe to the laws of Albertian perspective. Light entering a tiny hole in the wall of a darkened room, itself large enough for the artist to enter, would form an image on the wall opposite the hole, an image of whatever lay outside. Daniello Barbaro, professor at the University of Padua and author of *La practica della perspettiva* (1569), a treatise on perspective, suggested fitting the small hole with a lens:

Close all shutters and doors until no light enters the *camera* except through the lens,

and opposite hold a sheet of paper, which you move forward and backward until the scene appears in sharpest detail. There on the paper you will see the whole view as it really is, with its distances, its colors and shadows and motion, the clouds, the water twinkling, the birds flying. By holding the paper steady you can trace the whole perspective with a pen, shade it and delicately color it from nature.[9]

Space photographs are made by a process in which this *camera obscura* is metaphorically inverted, turned inside-out. Space itself is the "dark room" which contains within it both the intended target and the spacecraft, the moving "lens" that travels forward and backward until the scene appears in sharpest detail. And it is the surface of the Earth itself that is the sheet of paper, the plane on which you can see the whole view as it really is, with its distances, colors, shadows, and motion. The unmanned probes into deep space are conducted for the purpose of discovering our origins, our history, by charting our interrelationships with the universe. By holding the Earth steady, you can trace the whole perspective with a pen, shade it, and delicately color it from nature.

Christopher Knight

8. Roland Barthes, *Camera Lucida: Reflections on Photography* (New York, 1983), p. 9.

9. Daniello Barbaro, *La practica della perspettiva*, trans. A. Hyatt Mayor, in *Bulletin of the Metropolitan Museum of Art* (Summer 1946), p. 18.

Catalogue

The texts accompanying the photographs have been excerpted from interviews conducted by Jay Belloli, Director, Baxter Art Gallery, with Dr. Albert R. Hibbs, Office of Technology and Space Program Development, Jet Propulsion Laboratory, in January and February 1985; Donald J. Lynn, a consultant to the Image Processing Applications and Development Section, Jet Propulsion Laboratory, in March and April 1985; Catherine J. LeVine, Image Processing Applications and Development Section, Jet Propulsion Laboratory, in March 1985. The speakers are identified by their initials.

JB: How did the Jet Propulsion Laboratory get involved in the NASA program?

AH: We put up the first satellite. It was built here and launched on the front end of a Redstone missile. When NASA began, the only U.S. organizations that had really done something successfully in space were JPL and [Wernher] Von Braun's group at Redstone Arsenal. So we became part of NASA by presidential edict.

JB: From what I understand, you were under the Department of the Army prior to that. . . .

AH: Yes, we were part of the Army. Almost all of NASA was old NACA [National Advisory Committee on Aeronautics] laboratories that they took over. A portion of the Naval Research Laboratory that had been involved in Vanguard missile development was incorporated in NASA, and that became the Goddard Space Flight Center. They took Von Braun's group that was involved in missile design at Redstone Arsenal, and that became the Marshall Space Flight Center, and they took JPL.

JB: I assume the reason they approached you regarding Explorer 1 [launched January 31, 1958] is because for decades there had been rocket development going on here.

AH: Yes. In those days the joke was that the world had four space programs: there was the Russian space program, the Air Force space program, the Navy space program, and the Army space program. The International Geophysical Committee agreed, our armed forces representatives agreed, and so the Soviet representatives agreed that sometime in 1957-58 both countries would launch satellites. So then a committee was formed here in the United States called the Committee on Special Capabilities, chaired by Homer J. Stewart, who worked at JPL and was a professor at Caltech. That committee was to decide what should be undertaken in the United States program, and the only people who had the capability to do anything were the three

services. The Air Force was busy designing the Atlas at the time, and they also had the Delta; the Army had Redstone and was designing Jupiter; and the Navy was doing preliminary work for the Polaris. The committee asked each of the services to submit a proposal. The Air Force backed out saying that they would fly the first American in space in their Atlas, but just to put up a satellite on this short time schedule, they didn't want to be diverted from the Atlas development program. . . . The Navy and the Army then got into an interesting go-around, and the Navy won and was authorized to proceed with the Vanguard. The Army, however, was so convinced that the Navy would screw up that they went ahead anyway with their development of a satellite. . . . When the Vanguard finally failed after its second or third attempt — it blew up on the pad — the Army was asked by Eisenhower to prepare to launch a satellite, so we took all the stuff down to Florida, and it worked. We were sitting in pretty good shape to become part of NASA. When NASA was established by law, Congress gave the President the right to assign any other government-owned facilities to it within a year following. About six months later the president ordered the administration of the Redstone Arsenal and Jet Propulsion Laboratory facilities to be transferred from the Army to NASA along with the Caltech contract to manage JPL.

●

AH: We realized that things were going to change significantly when manned spaceflight began. NASA's obvious first job was to put a man up in space. We had the choice of either getting involved with that manned spaceflight project, [where] we would be a little frog in a very big puddle, or staying completely away from it, staying with unmanned flights and having a small puddle. There was a long series of arguments here, and at the same time we were reorganizing

JPL. For example, under the Army we had had no need to do scientific research. It wasn't our job; our job was to design and build guided missiles. But [William] Pickering [then the head of JPL] finally said, "We're going to have a scientific research organization here, and you're going to head it." So I became the first of the managers of the Space Science Division. Finally, we decided to stay out of the manned space business and concentrate on the unmanned.

JB: That decision would have been about 1959 or 1960?

AH: Yes, and we were already building the first of the lunar probes — the little Pioneers.

●

AH: When we decided to build these lunar probes [the Pioneers], we knew we would have to track them, and we thought, "As long as we are going to go into the unmanned exploration business, why not also go as far away from here as possible? Why not concentrate on planets?" So we gave this pitch to NASA, and NASA's response to this was, "It may be ten or twenty years before we do anything with the planets." To change their minds we put together a document on the exploration of the Moon and interplanetary space, and we took that to NASA. We had a lot of scientists involved. We presented the great challenge: Is there life on Mars? How were the planets formed? What is a comet? We addressed all these questions. It was a gorgeous plan that even had a mission to Mars occurring in the early '60s; all the programs that eventually came to be were in there. So NASA said, "All right, fine, you go that way, and we'll set up a Lunar and Planetary Office, but it will always be a small piece of the budget; the manned flights are going to take the big chunk." We accepted that, and we got into the lunar-planetary business and essentially abandoned Earth orbiters to Goddard. . . . So we began the first lunar flights and the first Venus flight, the first Mars flight.

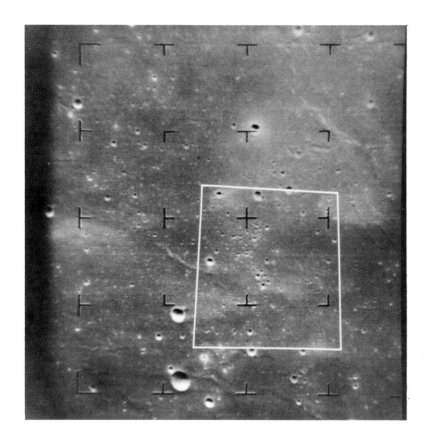

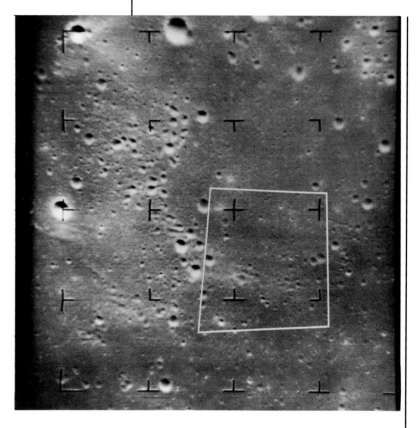

Editors' Note: The date at the end of each caption indicates when the image was originally created by the spacecraft. Initials following these dates indicate whether the original image is in black and white, color, enhanced color, or false color. For an explanation of relevant technical terms and processes, see the Appendix, pp. 116–119.

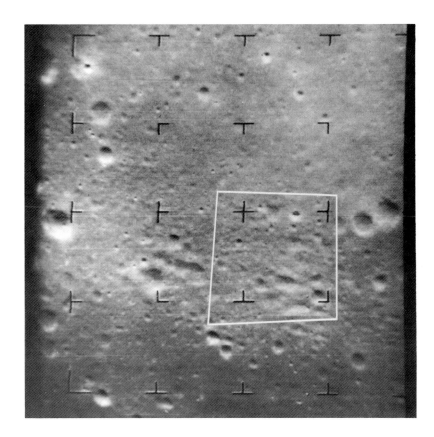

Wide-angle camera-A sequence from Ranger 7 during the last quarter-minute before impact on Mare Cognitum. 7/31/64 (B/W).

Final camera-P photograph from Ranger 7 showing noise after impact stopped image transmission. The photomosaic in the lower right is an area that has been enhanced to provide greater surface detail. 7/31/64 (B/W).

JB: From what I gather, there were problems getting the Ranger program going. The point was really to get a sense of what the surface of the Moon was like closer than you could see with a telescope — exactly what the terrain was like. Ranger was presumably tied in to the manned space program, so that you were gathering information for your own use and for their use later on.

AH: Maybe. They didn't think so. At least when the Apollo program started in the early sixties and the head of the Office of Space Sciences, Homer Newell, suggested that the Ranger and Surveyor programs were in support of Apollo, the Apollo program manager said, "Oh, is that so, then would you please give me the money." There was a lot of — not exactly bitterness. The Apollo people didn't like us hanging on their coattails and pointed out that before the Surveyor ever landed on the surface of the Moon to see how tough it was, they had already completed the design of the landing gear for Apollo.

●

AH: The launching rockets were very difficult, and the first two Rangers were lost because the rockets didn't work. They were supposed to go into orbit, a very high orbit, but they went into low orbit and burned up a short time. But the subsequent Rangers were failures also. We told NASA that we were going to build spacecraft that would stabilize themselves in space by looking at the Earth and the Sun; and we told them it had never been done before and they would have to be prepared for some failures. They didn't understand, and we didn't understand because under the Army everything we did had been secret. We didn't like failures, but at least they were private. But as soon as we were out in the public eye launching these extremely expensive Rangers that didn't work, the press and the Congress and everybody said, "What's wrong with you people, can't you ever

get anything to work?" So all of a sudden, the signals changed. We were forced to greatly revise our method of doing business, which resulted primarily in completely new procedures of documentation. Now a failure is a rarity, whereas before it was a fifty/fifty chance, or worse.

●

JB: Weren't specific sites chosen for Ranger to impact on? How were the decisions made as to where the Rangers were going to crash?

AH: Alphonsus has always been rather famous because many astronomers have reported lunar transient phenomena, LTP's, which look like smoke coming out of the surface of the Moon. The floor of the crater Alphonsus is a famous place for LTP's. Around that same crater are several small marks that can be seen from the Earth simply as small black circles, and it is suspected that they are carbon or some kind of cinder around volcanos, because they are quite unique and quite different from other areas. . . . We did get pictures of Alphonsus from one of the Rangers; the first time we could clearly see that inside those black halos there were definitely craters. They were so small. We didn't see any eruptions going on, but lunar transient phenomena are observed every few years.

JB: It's not like sunspots. There's no cycle; it just happens, and one hopefully sees it.

AH: We also wanted to look at areas called "the highlands," where there are a lot of craters all over the place and jumbled rocks. So we had several kinds of areas targeted for Ranger.

●

AH: The cameras were steadily improving all this time. When we started out, we wanted to use vidicon tubes. The older television cameras used were image orthicons; they were heavy and needed a lot of power. The vidicons were a new type of tube, but nobody could build a vidicon that you could tilt up without its insides falling

apart. They are extremely fragile. So we got together with RCA and redesigned a vidicon so that it would really be rugged. We got into the vidicon design business or at least worked very closely with these people. Those vidicons were the ones that flew in the Rangers, and derivatives of those were used all the way up through Voyager — continued improvements on those early vidicons.

●

JB: How does it work, Al?

AH: In those days it was very much like standard TV. A TV signal was received, which generated one line on the screen. And then the next line underneath it would be transmitted, and all these lines together would make the picture. With a regular TV signal these lines come so fast that you get 512, a complete picture, in one-thirtieth of a second. We didn't have enough power to send back a signal that fast. It would take a long time to send back a line, and if you looked at the TV screen, you would see one line at a time. So instead of trying to see these pictures on a TV receiver, we used the signal to draw one line at a time on photographic film, then looked at the picture when it was all complete.

JB: That's interesting, because when you got very close in and the impact occurred, you only got a partial image, which I guess would be partly a function of how slowly it was transmitted.

AH: Yes, Ranger often impacted right in the middle of a frame transmission.

●

JB: The image comes back with a lot of "noise," which I gather has to do with the machinery that creates the images disturbing the signal.

AH: No, it's just the nature of the signal. We get this very weak signal coming back from space, and signals from stars and so forth are mixed with it; we've got to figure out which of these signals we want. We can never really sort it out perfectly and totally clean it up.

JB: Basically, I've seen a sequence of four steps where you have the initial unprocessed image, and then a second image, almost like a grid, is superimposed on or drawn out of the first, a process which is, I guess, getting hold of the noise. The third image is basically just the grid pattern itself — presumably the extracted noise — and the fourth image is as close as you can get to what the original signal would have been.

●

JB: Then the information you got back from the Rangers is pretty much what you expected?
AH: I think so. We didn't expect the Moon to be quite so smooth. The only surprise was that when we got down to a close look, there were no really little craters. The smallest craters were a few feet across, and there were almost no smaller ones, so something had been sort of smoothing things out without making craters. The rate of covering was greater than the rate of cratering. Material dug up from one crater was covering up others, and the covering process was more efficient than the digging process. . . .

Photomosaic of lunar panorama near the Tycho crater taken by Surveyor 7. The hills on the center horizon are about eight miles away from the spacecraft. 1/68 (B/W).

JB: The Surveyors were the first soft-landing satellites, and they were designed to go to places that were being investigated as possible sites for Apollo.

AH: They were really chosen — well, both Surveyor and Apollo landing sites were chosen on the basis of their accessibility and their scientific interest. So in that sense we wanted to see craters, we wanted to see smooth areas, we wanted to see different kinds of rocks. . . . The Surveyors were to see what the Moon was made out of.

JB: Rather than to worry about where Apollo was going to come down.

•

AH: The Space Sciences Steering Committee for Surveyor and the Working Group on Lunar Exploration for Ranger argued as to exactly where we should target the landings, and they finally picked out the sites by committee process. . . .

JB: I didn't even think about the existence of committees. Clearly that's the way to make such decisions.

AH: You almost have to because there are too many different scientific arguments that have to be brought to bear. One person would have a tough time.

JB: What is the composition of the committee in terms of the types of scientists?

AH: Well, for the Lunar and Planetary Committee, for example, you first of all have people who are studying the planets. When we started the space program, there were no planetary astronomers trained in the United States. All of our planetary astronomers came from Europe. We had geologists, because we wanted to compare the Moon and planets to the Earth; geomorphologists, people who are concerned with impacting, meteorites, craters on the Moon; and some people who were interested in the effects of unfiltered sunlight that might take place over a period of time. So a variety of groups were represented.

AH: There was a lot of equipment on the original Surveyor design, and more weight than could be launched, so one instrument after another came off, until there were very few left. We were finally left with one camera (when there were originally supposed to be three), the alpha scattering experiment to measure the chemical constitution of the rocks, and a digging tool.

JB: The camera looked at the surface by means of a movable mirror.

AH: It couldn't look backwards through the structure, but we had an almost panoramic view. What we wanted was two cameras so we could get the stereo, like we have on the Viking landers. And there was supposed to be a down-pointing camera so you could get a view of the complete terrain as the Surveyor came down for its landing. It would have given us a map-like view of where it was landing so we could have known exactly where it was located.

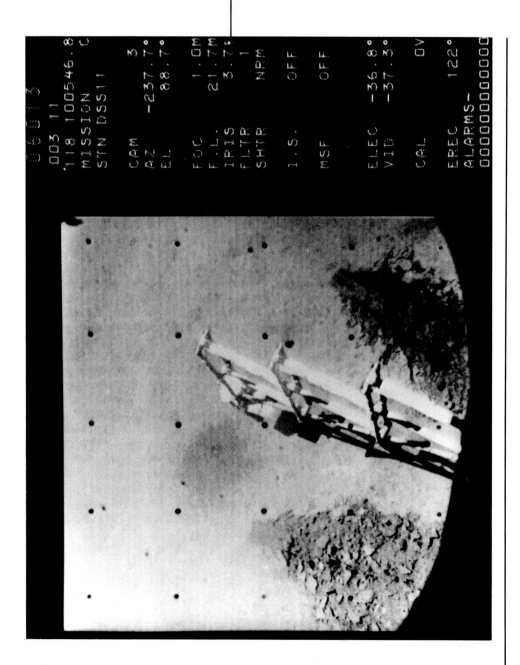

Remote-controlled surface sampler arm of Surveyor 3 after digging two trenches in the lunar surface of the Ocean of Storms. 4/28/67 (B/W).

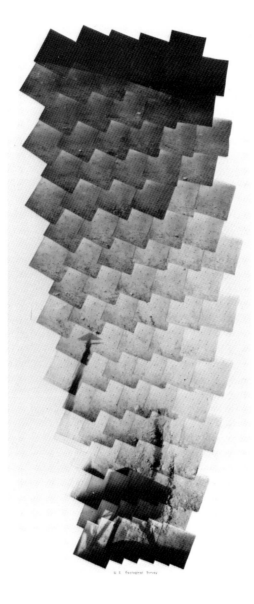

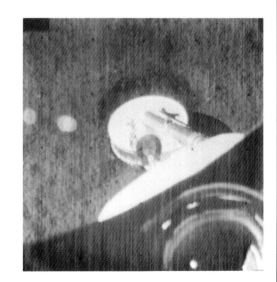

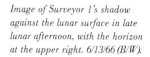

Image of Surveyor 1's shadow against the lunar surface in late lunar afternoon, with the horizon at the upper right. 6/13/66 (B/W).

Photomosaic of Surveyor 3 and the lunar horizon. 1967 (B/W).

Surveyor 1's foot resting next to its landing depression. White spots are reflections of the sun on lens elements; reflection of the filter wheel in the camera is visible at the lower right. 1966 (B/W).

JB: Mariner 10, the one that went by Mercury and Venus, that was the one that presumably started the color. . . .

AH: No, Surveyor did.

JB: Surveyor had color? I haven't seen any of those. All the Surveyor photos that I have seen are black and white.

AH: It was lousy color, but it was color, a filter wheel that could be rotated in front of the camera. The thing is, you know how colorful the Moon is.

JB: Yes.

AH: Dark brown.

JB: So it didn't do a whole lot.

AH: But there is one interesting color picture. There was a standard color disc on one of the Surveyor feet, and it is a picture with that color disc in the corner and the surface of the Moon behind it. The color scheme was just basically a situation where you get three different colors separated out . . . where it reads the three separate colors: red, green, blue, and then overlays them to get the final version. But we couldn't see any more on the Moon using color than we could in ordinary black and white, so we didn't bother with it too much.

View of the lunar surface from Surveyor 1. The image was obtained by photographic reconstruction using three color filters and three black and white negatives. 1966 (C).

JB: There were quite a few of the Surveyors, as I remember.
AH: Yes, seven.
JB: What exactly was found out by them?
AH: Well, the principal discovery was that the surface of the Moon was for the most part — where we went — like basalt and not like granite; it was like volcanic rock. . . . That was a primary result, and then there were the detailed nature and distribution of the material. Chemicals in that rock were somewhat different than in any Earth rock. That has been verified since by the Apollo samples, in much more detail, of course. The mechanical characteristics of the soil were measured by the scoop, and the scoop dumped some soil on some magnets that were attached to one of the legs. Some material stuck to the magnets, so we knew there was iron present.

Photomosaic of Earth's northern hemisphere taken by Surveyor 3 prior to an eclipse. The trace across this picture shows the line where the eclipse occurred; dotted lines show latitude and longitude. 4/23/67 (B/W).

Sunset on the Moon (seen upside down) photographed by Surveyor 2 from the Ocean of Storms. At the left is a blurred image of Surveyor's antenna boom. 6/14/66 (B/W).

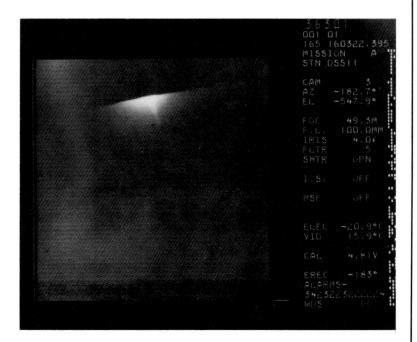

Photograph from Lunar Orbiter 4 of multi-ringed Orientale Basin, one of the youngest and best preserved of such areas on the Moon. The outer ring of the Cordillera Mountains is about 550 miles in diameter. 1967 (B/W).

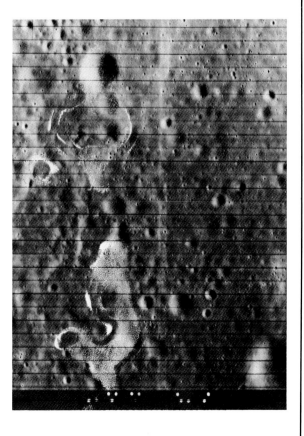

Photograph from Lunar Orbiter 3 of the horizon of the Moon. 1967 (B/W).

Photograph from Lunar Orbiter 2 showing an area of small craters. Dense dot patterns are imperfections in chemical processing of the film on board the spacecraft. 1967 (B/W).

JB: Lunar Orbiter was planned to go over certain positions on the Moon to pick up certain areas.

AH: It was to follow nearly a polar orbit and just stay in that orbit; the Moon turned around underneath it, and it photographed, photographed, photographed. Eventually it got just about the whole moon.

•

JB: The Lunar Orbiter was basically what? A Goddard program? JPL was involved in processing the photographs.

AH: It was a Langley [Research Center] program. JPL wasn't involved too much actually, but we did some work on the images.

JB: It's very strange because the setup at Langley was a photographic one. The Orbiters took photographs. They shot the images, developed the film, and transmitted the negatives to Earth by scanning them with an electron beam. And the electron beam worked just fine, but there are smudge marks on the negatives from the developing rollers. The whole procedure there was very peculiar in terms of what the vidicon did for the Ranger.

AH: It was Air Force-type camera equipment, not an independent NASA development. Also there is a rather odd thing that happened. It was supposed to be a mapping mission — straight down all the time — and a lot of the time they would leave the camera off for a long period because it was going over places that were already photographed. If you leave the camera off too long, the film tends to get sticky in the rollers, so it's necessary every now and then to take a picture whether or not you are interested

Photograph of Copernicus crater taken by Lunar Orbiter 2. The spacecraft was 45 miles above the surface. 1967 (B/W).

in the scene. One of those times, the controllers of the project decided to take a picture sideways instead of straight down; that's when they got that spectacular picture of Copernicus that's on everyone's wall. It was required by the mechanism of the camera that they take that picture. It wasn't because the scientists wanted it, and yet it became one of the most discussed pictures of the whole series.

JB: How often does that happen, Al? There seems to be a lot of . . .

AH: Playing around? It's easy to do when you get the data back here on Earth, and you're sitting poking buttons on the computer, but when you tilt the whole spacecraft around . . .

JB: So it doesn't happen that often in that particular way. Once the data comes in, *then* there is a lot of playing around.

First view of Earth from the Moon, photographed by Lunar Orbiter 1. The spacecraft was 730 miles above a portion of the Moon not visible from our planet. 8/23/66 (B/W).

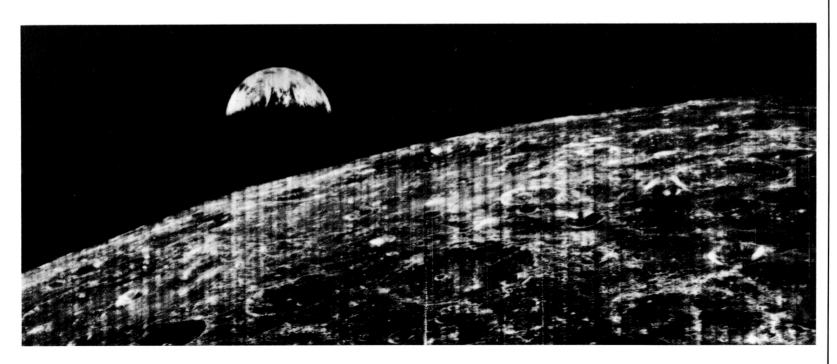

JB: How many projects were going on at once already in the early sixties? The Rangers started in '61 . . .

AH: We had Venus [Mariner 2] launched in '62, and Mariner 4 launched in '64 to Mars, and then all the other Mariners came very quickly after that.

JB: What was the lead time on all of this? I get the feeling that a lot of decisions were made very, very fast.

AH: Oh yes.

JB: As soon as you became a part of NASA?

AH: As soon as the president announced the decision to go to the Moon. All of a sudden money began to flow into NASA, and everybody's budget went up, not just the Apollo, so we really benefited from the Apollo.

JB: Which means that a lot of decisions were made for a lot of projects.

AH: Mariner 2 in '62 was the quickest one. I think we put that one together in eighteen months. That was just a Ranger fitted out to go to Venus. But of course we had designed Ranger to have planetary capability.

JB: Mariner 2, the Venus flyby, didn't take photographs but did do a whole lot of measurements.

●

AH: Mariner 2 was the first interplanetary flight. Then in '64 [Mariner 4] was the first Mars flight, and that was the one that got the first Mars pictures.

JB: Which were very, very limited, twenty-one pictures.

AH: We couldn't point the camera around, we didn't have enough time nearby. One pass across, that was all we got.

JB: You were still dealing with modified Rangers, then, if I'm following you correctly.

AH: Mariners are modified Rangers; they started out that way.

JB: So in terms of the image quality, it was the same basic setup you had on the Ranger.

AH: No, the cameras on the Rangers were put in that funny little tower, and there were six of them. The camera on the Mariner was sticking out of the bottom; there was only one, and it was pointed at a particular angle at the bottom, so that when Mariner flew by Mars with its solar panels pointed at the Sun and its star-sensor at Canopus, its camera was pointed at Mars. It had no scan-platform.

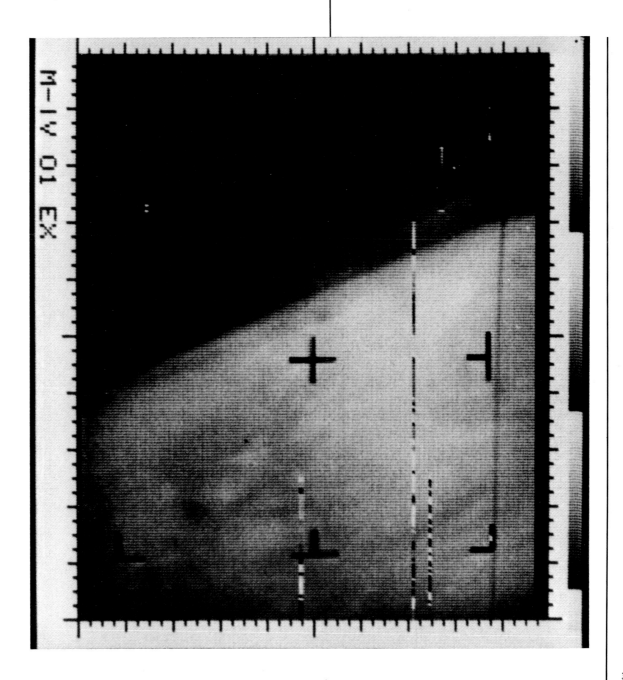

First picture of Mars (in "raw" state) from Mariner 4, taken through a red filter from approximately 10,500 miles away, showing Phlegra region and horizon. 7/14/65 (B/W).

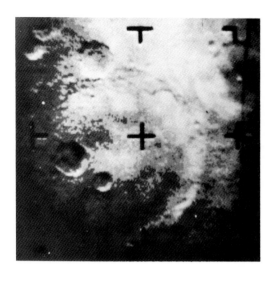

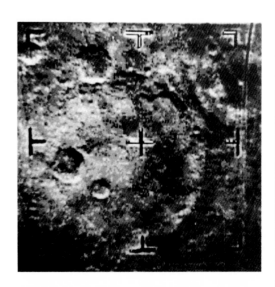

Eleventh picture of Mars from Mariner 4 (in "raw" state) taken through a green filter from 7,800 miles away, showing a crater seventy-five miles in diameter in the Atlantis region. 7/14/65 (B/W).

Eleventh picture of Mars after electronic noise from the spacecraft was removed. 1965 (B/W).

Eleventh picture of Mars after computer enhancement to present the highest definition of surface features. 1965 (B/W).

7F77 8/4/69 14.23.37 B CAMERA BOT GAIN 1.0
PHASE ANGLE 23 CENTRAL LONGITUDE 187 E
RANGE 374,919 KM
STRETCH - STRETCH - *NORING - *NOISREM - *DIFFPIC - BAND
DESTREAK - DESPIKE - DIFFPIC - SAR - SPKPIX - GEOM - GEOM3
LMICOR - STRETCH

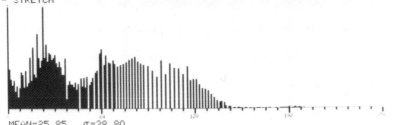

MEAN=25.85 σ=38.80

06-20-70 025640 JPL/IPL

JB: Were the Mars Mariners calibrated at particular points on the planet?

AH: Not the first Mars Mariner [Mariner 4] but after that, Mars flybys 6 and 7, which were launched in 1969, and the Mars orbiters, Mariners 8 and 9 [launched 1971]. The exact plans of those were definitely laid out. Mariner 7 went across the south pole, and Mariner 6 went across near the equator. Those two were just photographic flybys, but there were a lot of pictures in the flyby, a lot more than Mariner 4 could take.

View of the entire planet of Mars from Mariner 7, showing Nix Olympica (later identified as the giant shield volcano Olympus Mons) and polar caps, photographed from two hundred thousand miles away. 8/4/69 (B/W).

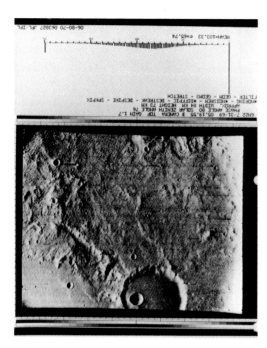

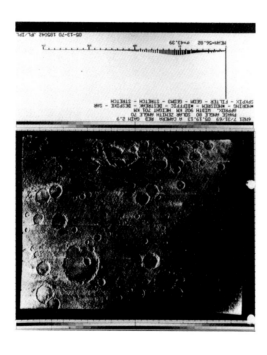

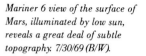

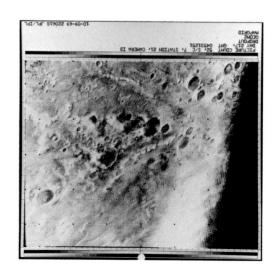

Mariner 6 view of the surface of Mars, illuminated by low sun, reveals a great deal of subtle topography. 7/30/69 (B/W).

Boundary between dark Sabaeus Sinus and light Deucalionis regions on Mars viewed by Mariner 6. There is no significant difference in crater distribution between light and dark areas. 7/30/69 (B/W).

View from Mariner 7 of the area immediately adjacent to the Martian south polar cap, showing ice at the lower right and a six-hundred-mile-long scalloped arc, which marks the extent of the winter ice cap. 8/4/69 (B/W).

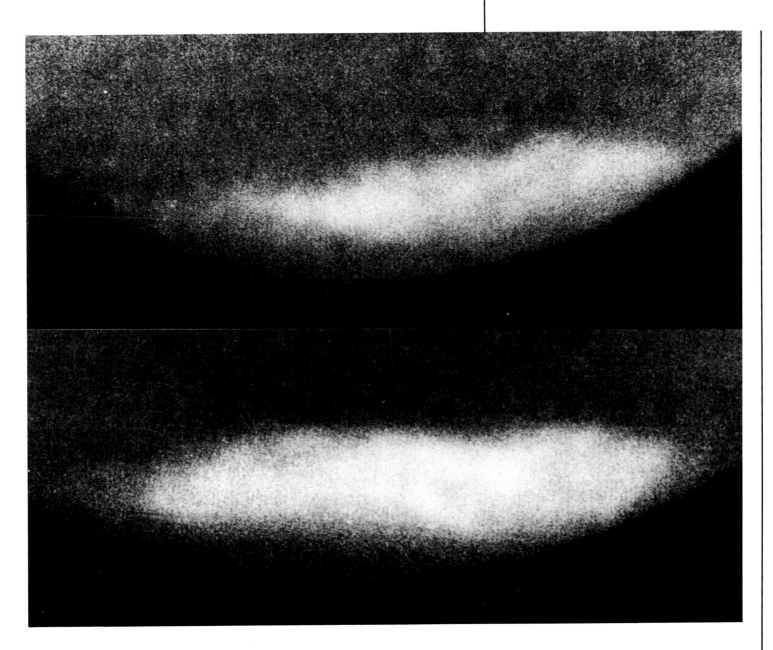

Enlarged views of Mars' south polar cap from Mariner 6. When first received, these two pictures, taken ninety degrees apart, were interpreted as suggesting that darkening toward the planet's edge might be caused by absorption of light in the Martian atmosphere. 7/30/69 (B/W).

Photomosaic from Mariner 9 of the northern hemisphere of Mars from the polar cap to south of the equator. Visible at the bottom, from left to right, are Olympus Mons, Tharsis Ridge, and the beginning of Valles Marineris. 8/7/72 (B/W).

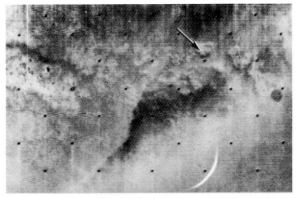

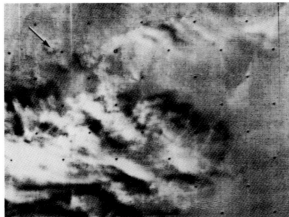

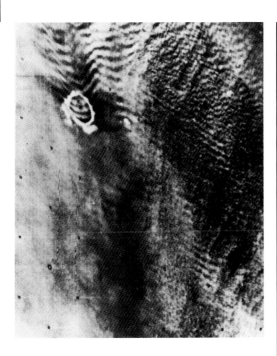

Views from Mariner 9 before, during, and after a three-hundred-mile-wide dust storm in the Euxinus Lacus region of Mars. The bottom photograph shows a dark surface increasingly exposed by the storm. 2/72 (B/W).

Winter carbon dioxide clouds in the Mare Acidalium region in Mars' northern hemisphere, photographed by Mariner 9. During this season, latitudes above about forty-five degrees N. are blanketed by clouds. 3/72 (B/W).

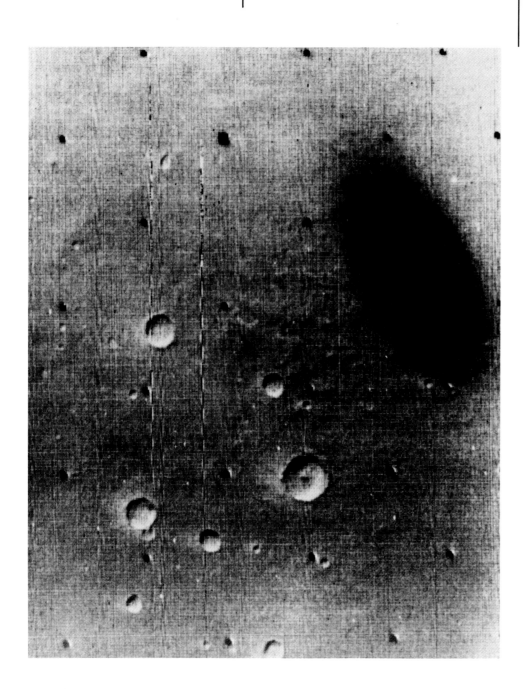

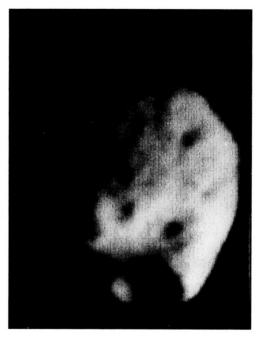

View from Mariner 9 of the shadow of one of Mars' tiny moons, Phobos, on the planet's Aethiopis region. Phobos is the innermost of the Martian moons and is a craggy oval thirteen by sixteen miles in size. 2/4/72 (B/W).

View of Phobos from Mariner 9. Visible at the bottom is the Stickney crater. 1972 (B/W).

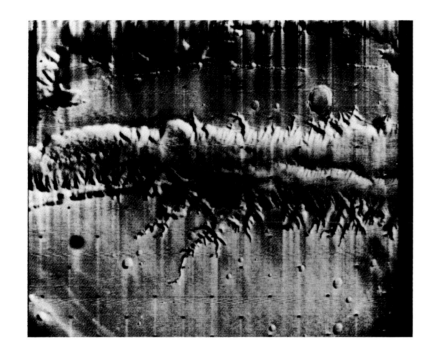

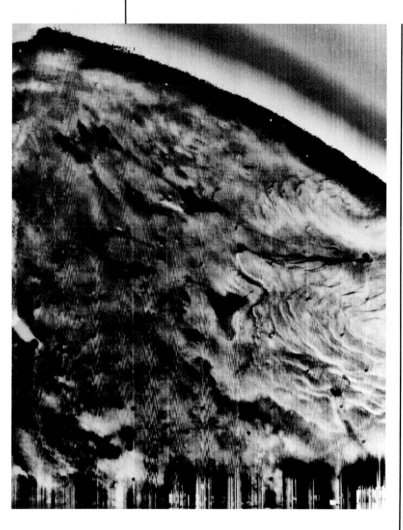

View from Mariner 9 of the vast chasm on Mars, Valles Marineris, with branching canyons. Valles Marineris would span the distance from San Francisco to New York and averages almost three miles in depth. 1/12/72 (B/W).

Oblique view from Mariner 9 of north polar ice cap of Mars, showing circular land forms similar to those at Martian south pole. Visible within the polar cap is layered terrain, the most significant feature of the polar regions. 6/72 (B/W).

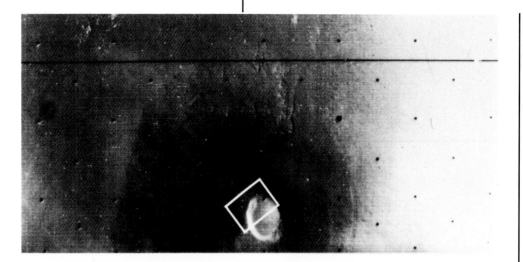

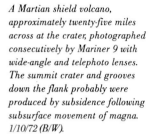

A Martian shield volcano, approximately twenty-five miles across at the crater, photographed consecutively by Mariner 9 with wide-angle and telephoto lenses. The summit crater and grooves down the flank probably were produced by subsidence following subsurface movement of magna. 1/10/72 (B/W).

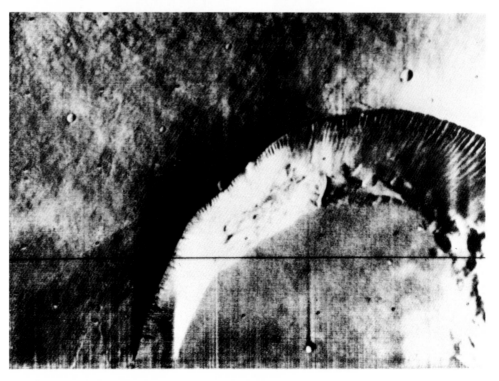

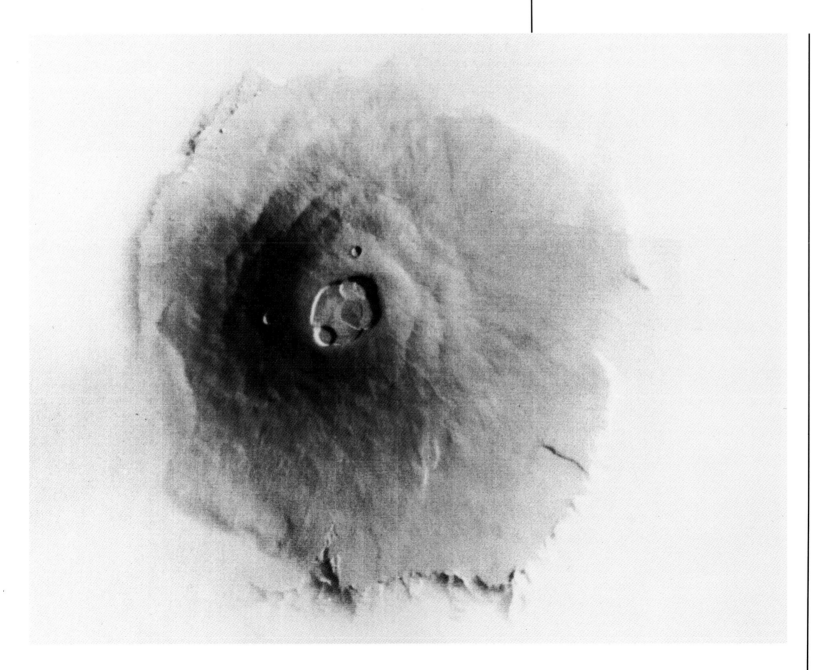

Olympus Mons photographed by Mariner 9. 435 miles across at the base and over eighty thousand feet high, Olympus Mons is the largest known volcano in the solar system and is more than twice as broad as the most massive volcanic pile on Earth. Late 1/72 (B/W).

JB: Mariner 9 did exactly the areas that people were interested in. In terms of Mariner 10, was there that same amount of control over what was going to be looked at on Venus?

AH: The path past Venus was chosen for gravitational reasons because Mariner 10 had to do exactly the right change . . .

JB: To get to Mercury?

AH: To get to Mercury; it was the first spacecraft to use the gravity of one planet to get to another. The scientists had little choice as to where they were going past Venus.

JB: So what they got, in a sense, was what they could get as they went by.

AH: Which was pretty good.

JB: In the Mercury situation, there were three passes, I gather. Something interesting happened there where some other mission was occurring at the same time and the amount of information that could be brought in on Mercury was not everything that the Mariner 10 was picking up. The thing that fascinated me was that as a result, what you found out about Mercury is not as complete as it might have been. Basically it shows one side of the planet.

AH: Unfortunately, that's the way the cycles work. Each time we went by Mercury, it was at the same part of its orbit and with the same face to the Sun.

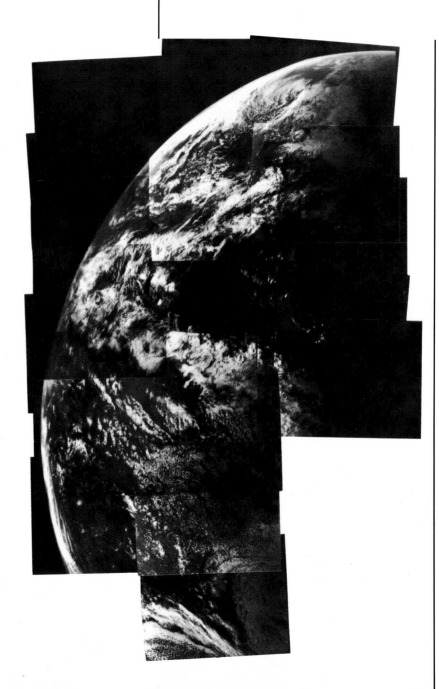

Photomosaic of Earth from Mariner 10 made during camera calibration tests as the spacecraft began its journey to Venus and Mercury. 11/3/73 (B/W).

JB: On Mariner 10 there was a fairly full complement of filters and yet, because of the nature of Venus, the ultraviolet filter was used and, because of the nature of Mercury, which was colorless, black and white was used. In other words, there was more hardware there than was really utilized.

AH: We took color pictures of Mercury, but they didn't show anything.

JB: And didn't show up different than black and whites basically.

AH: Because of the cost restrictions on the Mariner 10, we did not have two vidicons — we didn't have both the telephoto and the wide-angle. Instead, we had what was called a wide-angle filter — the WAF — so that the wide-angle lens was like one you might stick on in front of your own camera . . . a clip-on lens to turn an ordinary lens into a wide-angle one. Of course, that meant we couldn't use color filters and the wide-angle lens at the same time. There was only one filter wheel.

JB: On journeys previous to Mariner 10, were there situations where both wide-angle and telephoto lenses were used?

AH: That was standard, and it was also the case on Voyager.

JB: Standard, from how early on, roughly, just from the Mariner program?

AH: Mariner 6, 7, 8, 9, but not 10.

View from Mariner 10, taken with an ultraviolet filter, of Venus' cloud cover, printed in blue to simulate ultraviolet light. Sequences of images such as this one provided information about the rotation of the atmosphere around the planet. 2/74 (FC).

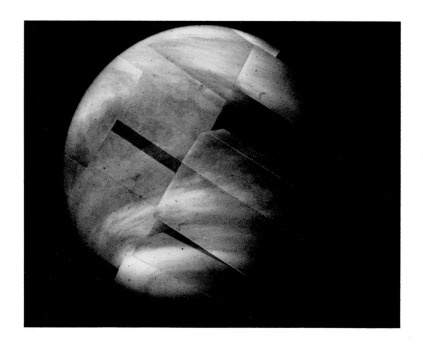

Photomosaic of Venus from Mariner 10. A wealth of atmospheric detail, invisible to the naked eye, is revealed by this ultraviolet image. 2/74 (B/W).

Cloud cover of Venus from Mariner 10, photographed from 490,000 miles away. Cells of rising air in Venus' subsolar region can be seen in this ultraviolet image. 2/5/74 (B/W).

Mosaic of photographs of Mercury taken by Mariner 10 from 125,000 miles away. The tiny, brightly rayed crater (just below center top) was the first recognizable feature on the planet's surface and was named in memory of astronomer Gerard Kuiper, a Mariner 10 team member. 3/29/74 (B/W).

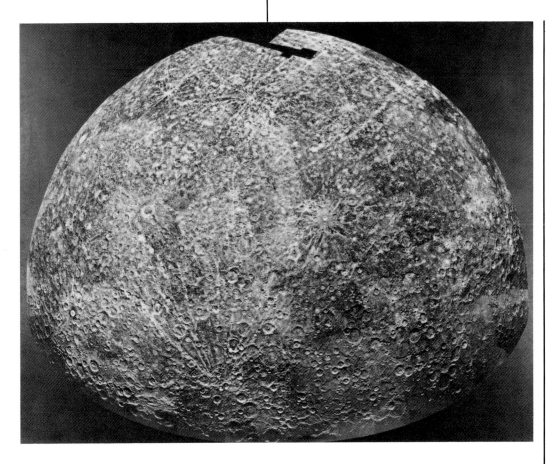

South polar region of Mercury from the second Mariner 10 flyby. The photograph shows that the land forms in the polar region are the same as those on the rest of the planet. The large crater at center bottom exactly marks the south pole. 9/74 (B/W).

Many Mariner 10 photographs were specially computer-processed to create this view of Mercury's southern hemisphere. The south pole is located in the large crater at the bottom of the photograph. 1975 (B/W).

JB: Has the technology improved since Ranger?

AH: Yes, image-processing technology is much better. When we transmit a picture, we break each line up into about a thousand little squares called pixels. So instead of looking at the strength of the signal to determine how dark a spot is, we send a number from zero to 255.

JB: When did that come into being?

AH: Mariner 4.

JB: And so you now get a number for each one of those pixels, and the computer really does have to come in and say, "That number means gray, a little grayer, a little darker, a little lighter." And the result is that you can get a lot of information faster.

AH: You can get a lot better information about the shade of gray in the object that you are looking at — it's called dynamic range. With the old system the difference between completely dark and completely light, the degree to which you could tell one point from another point, was only ten or fifteen levels. If the scenes were particularly dark, you'd get a signal that would be almost black with little spots of gray in the middle every now and then. Now, we know that the human eye can't see 255 shades of gray, but we still transmit all that information. For example, often the first picture we see will look absolutely light; you can't see anything. Saturn came in so bright we couldn't see any features. But with a computer, we translate the data. The eye can't tell the difference between the brightest ten or fifteen shades out of 256. But the computer makes, say, number 240 look like 0, 241 like 15, 242 like 30, and so on. Then a picture that looked all white to begin with now has a complete range — to the eye — from black to white. All the details are visible.

This Mariner 10 photomosaic shows a large impact basin on Mars called Caloris, which is located at one of the two spots on Mercury that face the Sun at the planet's closest approach to it. 1975 (B/W).

After passing on the dark side of the planet, Mariner 10 photographed the other, somewhat more illuminated, hemisphere of Mercury. The north pole is at the top, two-thirds down from which is the equator. 3/29/74 (B/W).

Photo taken as Viking Orbiter 2 approached the Martian dawn, showing the giant volcano Ascreaus Mons, with water-ice cloud plumes, and the immense canyon Valles Marineris. Early 8/76 (EC).

JB: My instincts tell me that almost every image that finally gets printed as a photograph is an enhanced image.

DL: Yes.

JB: I mean it's simply not showing it as it is.

DL: Sometimes it is. Mercury, for instance, was a very high contrast black and white image. That didn't take much enhancement for many of the images. On the other hand, when Mariner 9 arrived at Mars, there was very little contrast and you couldn't see anything without enhancement.

JB: But if you have something like Jupiter, or Saturn with the bands . . .

DL: Which have very low contrast; they require enhancement. Also Uranus . . . we expect Uranus to look like a billiard ball without some very strong enhancements.

JB: Here you get into the whole relationship between what's out there and what you are doing. The enhancements are used to understand what is going on there. So what goes on there is really not what you get.

DL: That's right. Viking was the first planetary mission with color carefully planned. If you say, "I want to see real color; let's see what that would look like, that rock," then you get into these questions: "Do you want to know what that rock would look like to you if you were standing on Mars? Do you want to know what that rock would look like to you if you saw it in Earth's atmosphere? Do you want to know what that rock looks like with no atmosphere at all?" You have all these questions which must be addressed before you produce the picture.

JB: A lot of Viking photographs seem to be what it would look like if you were on Mars, because you get that pink blush in the atmosphere.

DL: Not all of them, because some of the scientists wanted to look at the rocks and see if they looked familiar; they wanted to know what the rocks would look like in an Earth atmosphere. Some of the initial images were done that way,

but the later pictures tended to show the scene as it appeared on Mars.

JB: Yes, pinkish. It kind of starts getting that blush that you get with original Technicolor where there were three sheets of film, because you are dealing with overlays and so you can't get complete definition.

DL: But even with your color films — like Kodachrome — it's not real color; it's the spectacular color that people want to see. Most of the color pictures you see from Voyager are color enhanced, but it is important to differentiate color enhancement from pseudocolor. With pseudocolor the colors don't bear any relationship to actual color.

JB: And it's done to see certain details of a geological or chemical nature, or whatever.

DL: That's right. Different colors are used to greatly accentuate what may be only small differences in intensity or color in the original scene.

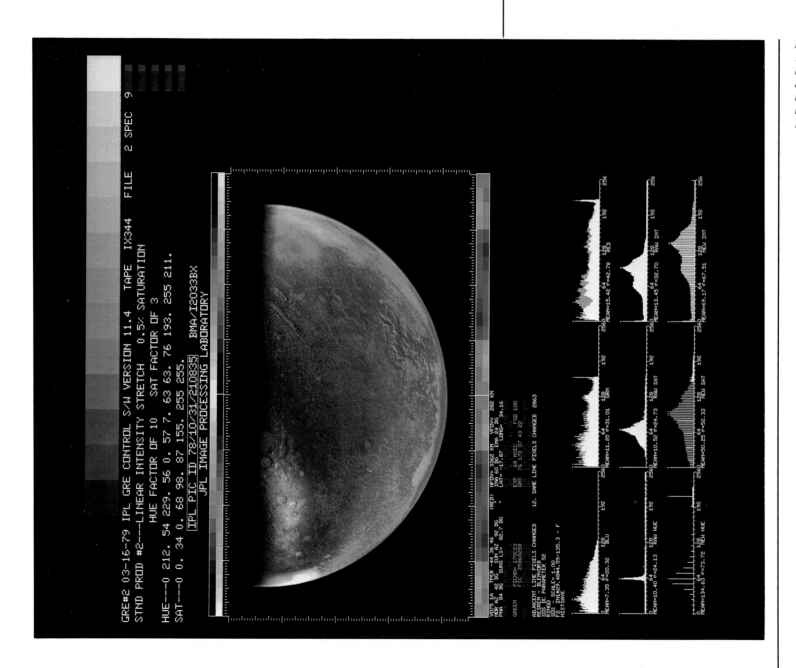

Photograph from Viking Orbiter 1, showing the Martian hemisphere with the south polar cap on the bottom. Above, near the line between day and night, is the large impact basin Argyre Planitia. 10/31/78 (FC).

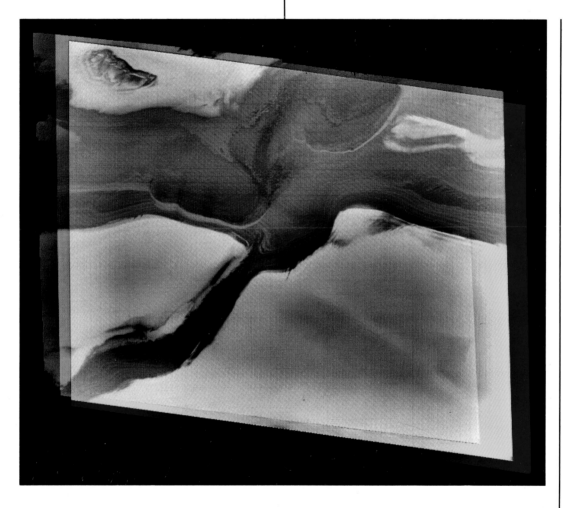

Photo of the surface of Mars from Viking Orbiter 1 showing the Martian carbon dioxide atmosphere. Several high-altitude cloud layers are visible on the horizon. The large basin, Argyre Planitia, was made by an asteroid impact. 7/76 (EC).

South Martian polar cap seen by Viking Orbiter 2 in mid-summer when the carbon dioxide ice melts to reveal water-ice and the layered terrain beneath. This picture shows how black and white photographs taken through colored filters are combined to create a color image. 10/27/76 (EC).

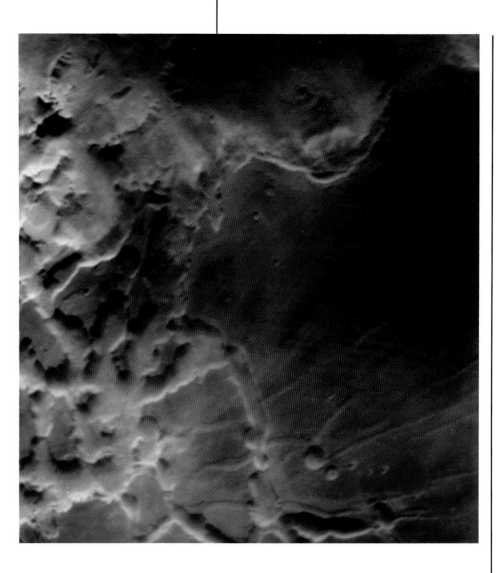

The eastern portion of Valles Marineris surrounded by the Ridged Plains in Viking Orbiter photograph. The faults just south of the valley are believed to have resulted from slumping of the canyon walls. 10/77 (EC).

The water-ice clouds shown in this Viking Orbiter 1 photograph form in the early morning in the small canyons of the high plateau region of Mars called Noctis Labyrinthus. 7/76 (EC).

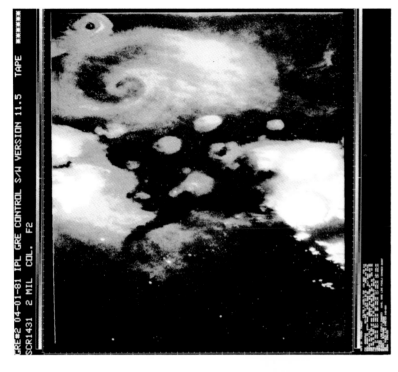

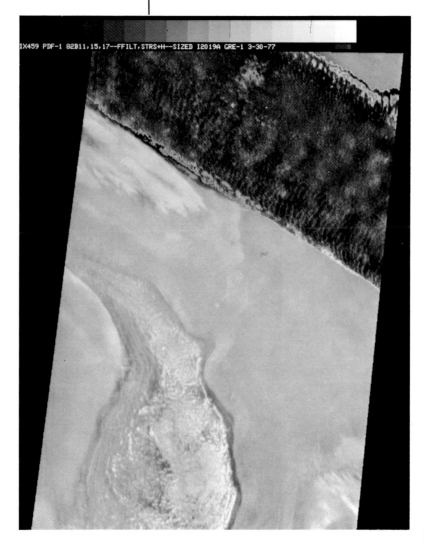

View from Viking Orbiter 1 of a Martian storm near the north polar front. The clouds seen in storm fronts such as this are made up of water or water-ice like those on Earth. 8/9/78 (FC).

A photomosaic from Viking Orbiter 2 showing, at its smallest size, the melting Martian north polar cap of frozen carbon dioxide and water. The dark bands, exposed layered terrain devoid of ice, spiral toward the cap's center. 8/30/76 (B/W).

Photograph from Viking Orbiter of the Martian south polar cap showing the ice and layered terrain. (EC).

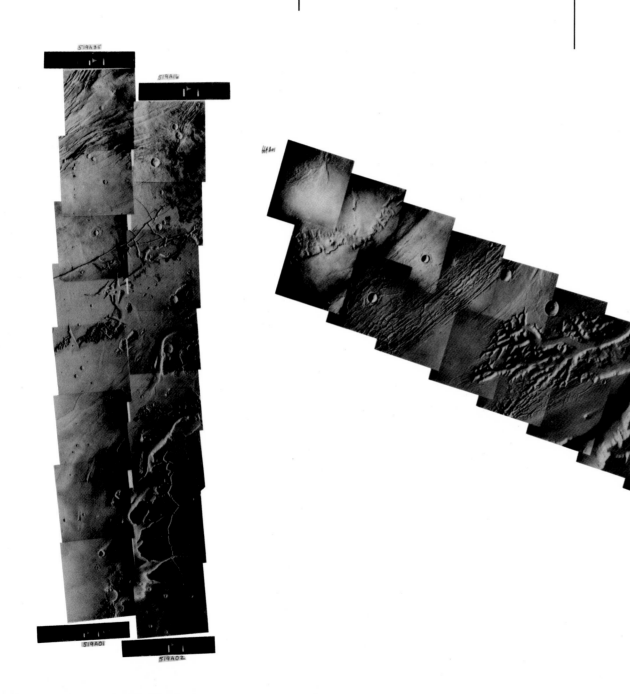

Photomosaic from a high orbit of Viking Orbiter showing the Lunae Palus area of Mars and its wide variety of surface terrain. 11/18/77 (B/W).

Photomosaic from a low orbit of Viking Orbiter showing the Kasei Vallis area of Mars, including a section of the previous photograph of the Lunae Palus area. 1977 (B/W).

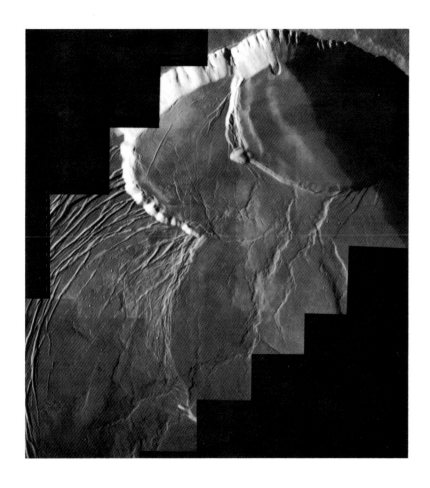

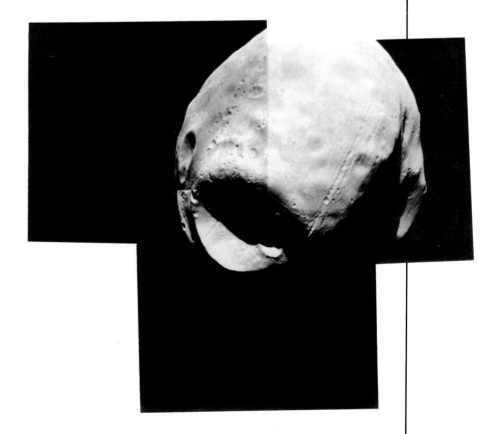

Viking Orbiter 1 photomosaic of the Olympus Mons summit caldera. The caldera comprises a series of craters formed by repeated collapses after eruptions. 6/13/77 (EC).

Photomosaic from Viking Orbiter 1 of Phobos from 380 miles away. Linear grooves coming from and passing through Stickney crater at the bottom appear to be fractures caused by the impact that formed the crater. 10/19/78 (B/W).

Among the sharpest photographs of the surface of Mars from Viking Lander 1, this view shows numerous rocks and a dune field similar to many seen in the deserts of Earth. The meteorology boom that supported Viking's miniature weather station cuts through the picture's center. 8/3/76 (B/W).

Photomosaic from Viking Lander 2 of the Martian landscape, looking toward the northeast horizon two miles away. The photograph is angled because the spacecraft landed with one footpad on a rock and was tilted eight degrees. 9/76 (B/W).

The surface sampler arm on *Viking Lander 2* pushing a rock to collect a soil sample. The sample was sought from beneath a rock because it was believed that, if there were life forms on Mars, they might seek rocks as shelter from the Sun's intense ultraviolet radiation. *10/8/76 (B/W).*

Photograph that *Viking Lander 2* took of itself showing its color calibration wheel and the American flag. The northwest horizon is in the background below the pink Martian sky. *1976 (EC).*

Martian sunset over Chryse Planitia taken by Viking Lander 1 during a ten-minute period. The blue-to-red color variation is explained by a combination of scattering and absorption of sunlight by atmospheric particles. 8/20/76 (EC).

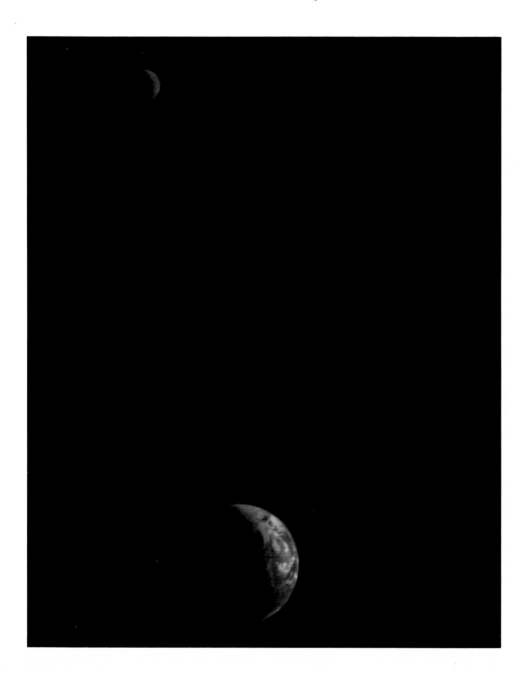

First photograph of the Earth and Moon together, taken by Voyager 1 on its way to Jupiter from a distance of seven-and-a-quarter miles. Since the Moon is much darker than the cloudy Earth, its image has been brightened. 1977 (EC).

Jupiter, Io (over the planet's surface), and Europa are seen in this Voyager 1 photograph. Many Jovian storm systems are visible, including the Great Red Spot. 2/13/79 (EC).

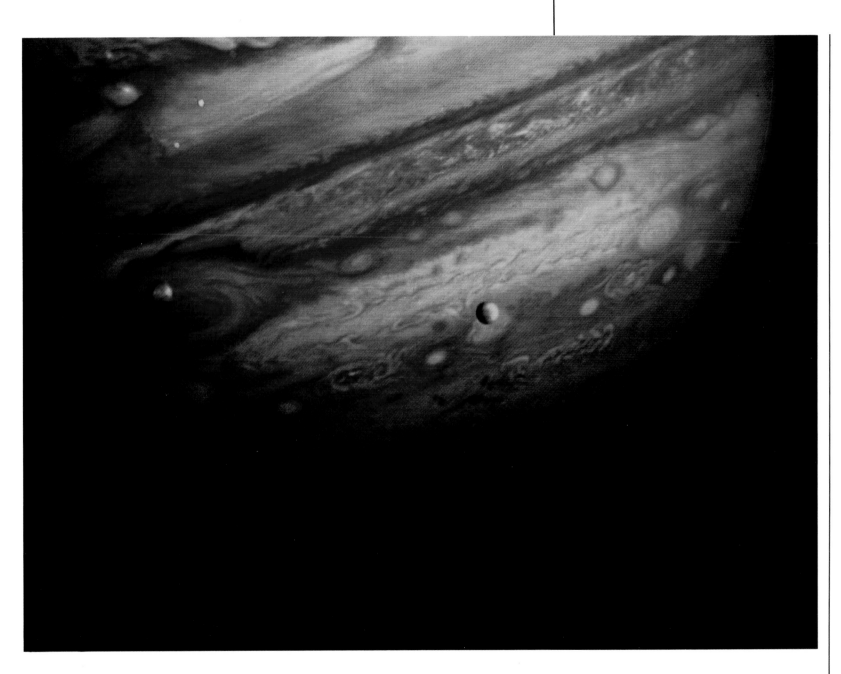

Seen from a distance of twelve million miles are the inner and smaller two of Jupiter's satellites observed in the seventeenth century by Galileo, Io (left) and Europa, passing in front of Jupiter. 2/13/79 (EC).

Jupiter

AH: The major change in technology for Voyager was the much greater capability of its computers — its on-board computers. Instead of sending separate commands, we send a complete program to its computer. Then we can, for example, run its program through a dummy Voyager to make sure it wasn't going to give any trouble.

JB: So that in terms of the aim of the probe, just about anything . . .

AH: You can tell it to send various kinds of data back, send this data instead of that data, stop sending data that we don't need, whatever, or send more engineering data. It is sensing and picking up an awful lot more than it sends us, particularly about the condition of its own various engineering measurements. And normally, we turn it down to a very low rate and just pay attention to things that look unusual. It has little scales on each instrument, and it checks against the scale. It will interrupt and tell us if we've got an unusual reading.

JB: Now you have what you are expecting to see built into the system, and as soon as something else comes up, it will switch to that.

•

JB: I think people in general, that is, I believed that a lot of what was coming back was dealt with in terms of the imaging to make it look exactly like the planet. That's not the issue at all. It's done to find out things about the planet, not in terms of visual aspect.

AH: Sometimes both. Sometimes the image team is just so fascinated with what they have accomplished when they have played around, that they think not only is that useful, but beautiful; and maybe we could do a little more, stretch it a little more, like the bumblebee picture of Saturn; you have seen that.

JB: Yes, blue and orange.

AH: That was art, and nothing extra was learned scientifically. It was just beautiful. But

enhancing the cloud structure of Jupiter was to bring out details in the vortexes; it was sort of mucky in the original color.

•

JB: In terms of what was discovered from Voyager, besides the volcanos on Io, there was some manifestation of the rings of Jupiter that was not expected. What were the other major discoveries on those two missions?

AH: I think quite a bit was discovered — new moons around Saturn certainly, and the rather curious dynamics of the Saturnian moons, and the interaction with the rings; a better look at the surface of the moons, particularly the curious nature of Europa.

JB: How is it curious?

AH: It's flat. Absolutely smooth. I shouldn't say it's flat, it's round, but smoother than the smoothest possible ball bearing. Everything else is all covered with craters, but not Europa. It's a smooth ball of ice, which implies that underneath the ice is liquid water. The nature of the marks on Callisto and Ganymede . . . those marks are a little odd too. We discovered a lot of new mysteries, of course, and the icy moons of Saturn are just delightful; one of them has a great crater, almost as big as the moon itself.

•

JB: What is expected in terms of Uranus? In fact, where is Voyager 2 now? There are images being given. At this distance, are they able to calibrate fairly much where it goes by?

AH: Yes.

JB: Still, I think you described it as kind of a geriatric probe at this point.

AH: It has arthritis, it's hard of hearing, and it's a little senile, but that doesn't change its trajectory through space. Isaac Newton fixed that for us.

JB: Project plan for Neptune is how many years further on?

AH: 1989, four years away. But the science objectives for Neptune are probably the same

Jupiter

mission objectives. They're very bland. . . . Look at the atmosphere, look at the satellites, see if there is anything new we haven't seen before. It's the surprises that really count.

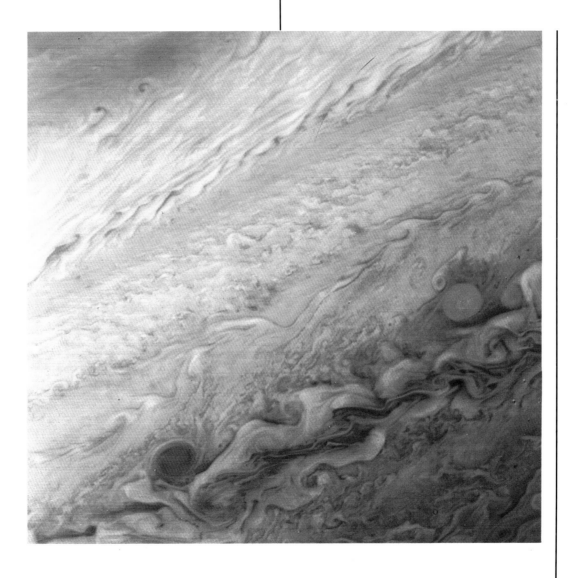

High-resolution photograph taken by Voyager 1 of finely detailed weather patterns in Jupiter's northern hemisphere. The pale orange straight line marks a jetstream with speeds of about 270 miles per hour. 3/2/79 (EC).

69

Jupiter

Jupiter's ring sparkles as Voyager 2 looks back at the dark side of the planet. The visible portion of the ring disappears when it enters Jupiter's shadow. 8/11/79 (FC).

A photograph from Voyager 2 of Jupiter and its ring taken from inside the planet's shadow. Jupiter is outlined by sunlight scattered from a haze layer high in the atmosphere. 7/10/79 (EC).

Jupiter

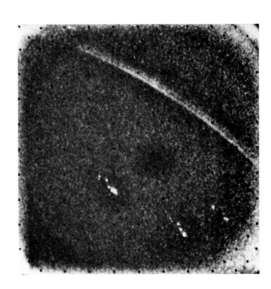

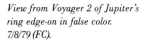
View from Voyager 2 of Jupiter's ring edge-on in false color. 7/8/79 (FC).

A double auroral arc in the north polar region of Jupiter photographed by Voyager 1. Below the aurora are numerous flashes of lightning illuminating the clouds. 3/5/79 (B/W).

Although the Voyagers did not fly over Jupiter's poles, it was possible to construct this image of the south pole from existing photographs. Unlike the rest of the planet, the polar areas do not show strongly banded structures. 1979 (EC).

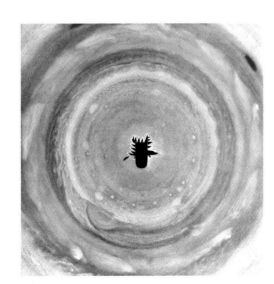

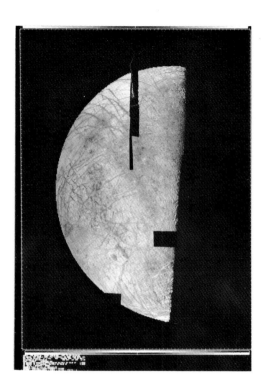

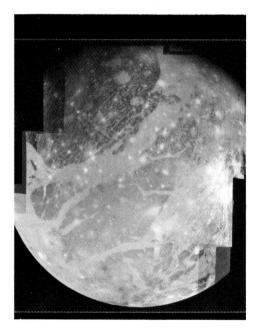

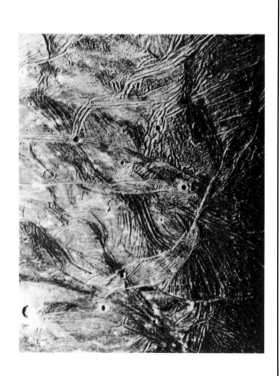

Photomosiac of Europa from Voyager 2, showing fractures in its icy surface filled with dark material from below. The dark streaks are about six miles wide. 7/9/79 (EC).

Photomosaic of Jupiter's largest moon, Ganymede, from Voyager 2. Many dark areas are heavily cratered. Other features resulted from intense internal geologic activity. 1979 (EC).

The surface of Ganymede from Voyager 1 showing an area of geologic activity. These areas consist of many parallel lines of mountains and valleys intersected by what appear to be fault-like discontinuities. 3/5/79 (B/W).

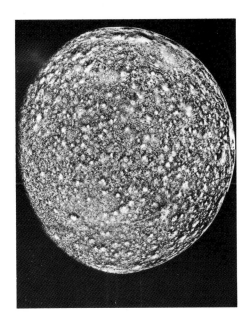

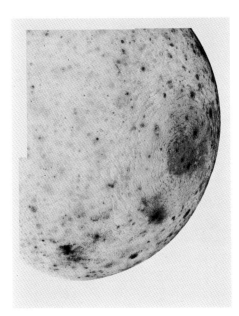

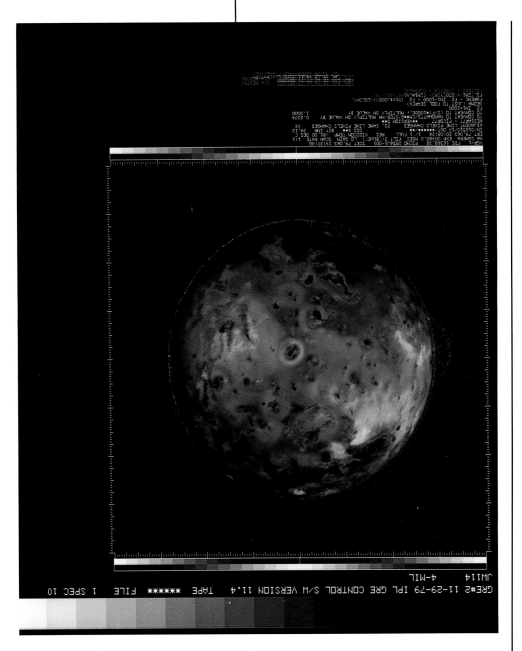

Photograph from Voyager 2 of Jupiter's second-largest moon, Callisto, showing the extensive and uniform distribution of impact craters. Most recent bombardment is evident in craters that are surrounded by bright rays, which are fresh ice on the older, darker surfaces. 7/8/79 (B/W).

Photomosaic of Callisto. Because the impact craters formed in an icy surface, many of the larger ones have nearly returned to their original level. 3/6/79 (EC).

View of Io from Voyager 1. Volcanoes and lava lakes cover the landscape and continually resurface it, so that any impact craters have disappeared. 11/17/79 (EC).

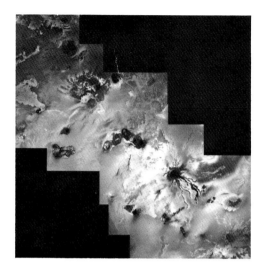

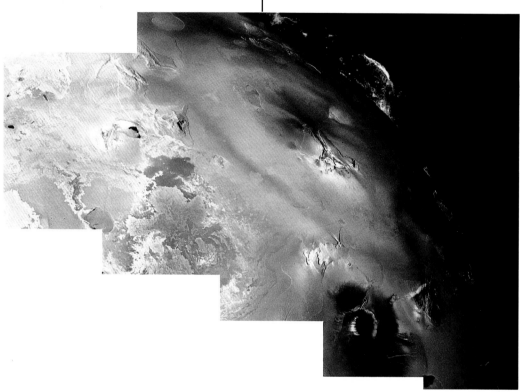

Photomosaic of Io from Voyager 1 showing results of volcanic activity. 3/79 (FC).

Photomosaic of Io taken by Voyager 2, showing the first volcanic activity seen beyond Earth. The volcano Pele hurls ejecta 175 miles above the surface. Io is the most volcanically active body known in the solar system. 3/79 (FC).

Io's south polar regions seen by Voyager 1. A variety of terrains are visible, including mountains over six miles high. 3/5/79 (FC).

Jupiter

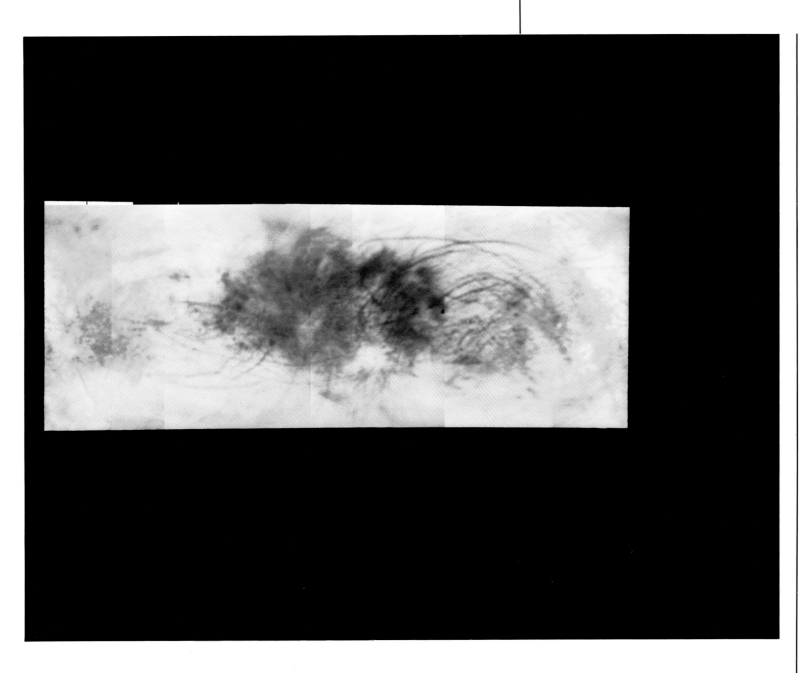

Image of Europa's surface from Voyager 2, made for mapping purposes. 1979 (EC).

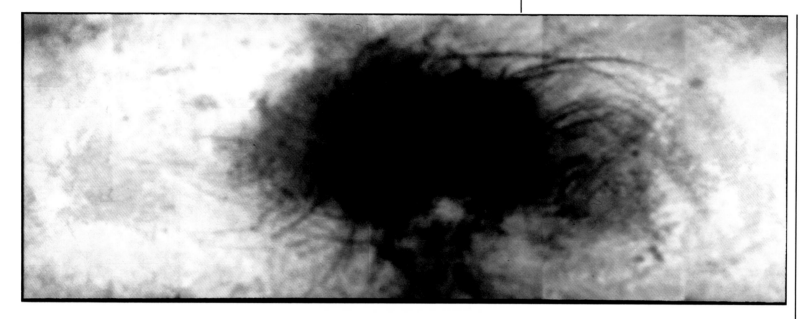

Surface of Europa from Voyager 2. 1979 (FC).

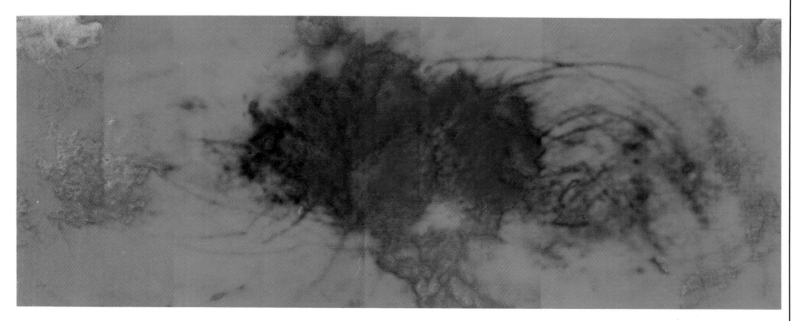

Jupiter

Image from Voyager 2 of Jupiter's moon Europa, the smallest of the planet's Galilean satellites. The surface consists primarily of uniformly bright terrain, mainly water-ice. 8/8/79 (EC).

Saturn photographed by Voyager 1 as it sped away from the planet. The planet's shadow falls on the rings from a perspective never before seen. 11/16/80 (EC).

A large atmospheric storm in Saturn's north latitudes photographed from 620,000 miles away by Voyager 2. The darker, bluish area in the upper right, oriented east to west, suggests the presence of a jetstream. 8/25/81 (FC).

Saturn's southern hemisphere from Voyager 1 at a distance of 5.3 million miles, showing a unique red oval cloud. It is similar to Jupiter's Great Red Spot, but only 1,850 miles in diameter. 11/6/80 (FC).

DL: On the Voyager spacecraft, there are two cameras, one "wide angle" with a 300mm lens, and one "narrow angle" with a 1500mm lens. In these cameras, the imaging sensor is a vidicon — similar to a normal TV camera, except that it has a slow scan tube. That is, it reads out the image at a much slower rate than a normal TV camera. It takes the Voyager camera forty-eight seconds to read out a full frame instead of one-thirtieth of a second, like a normal TV camera. Also, the Voyager image size is eight hundred lines by eight hundred samples, and the image is digitized within the camera electronics.

JB: On the spacecraft itself?

DL: Yes, the camera produces a stream of digital data that represents the picture. This data is fed to the data system on the spacecraft, which embeds it in the downlink telemetry stream back to Earth, or records it on the on-board tape recorder. From Uranus, we can't transmit data from the spacecraft to the Earth with enough power to send it at 115.2 kilobits per second — that is the real-time data rate that would be required to transmit a full image in real time. The highest data rate that the system can support with all of the stations arrayed and all the bells and whistles going is around 29.9 kilobits per second. That means that the data rate coming from the camera must be slowed down by about a factor of four. Now there are a variety of ways to do that; one is to put the data on a tape recorder.

JB: Here? When it comes back?

DL: There are two tape recorders on board the spacecraft which can record at 115.2 kilobits right out of the camera and then play the tape back at a slower rate. So the downlink data rate can be slowed down to, oh, 7.2 kilobits, but then it takes sixteen times longer to get a full frame down.

JB: Which would be close to twelve minutes or something like that.

DL: Right. So that greatly limits the number of frames that can be transmitted to Earth during the encounter. Another thing that can be done is

Saturn and two of its moons, Tethys (above) and Dione, photographed by Voyager 1 from eight million miles away. In the shadow cast by the rings on the bland, almost featureless planet, sunlight can be seen streaming through the Cassini Division and another gap. The shadow of Tethys is also visible at lower right. 11/3/80 (EC).

Saturn

to play out partial frames, instead of sending whole frames back. For instance, there are a couple of different edit modes where they send down a portion of the frame, or they can send it back "slow scan," where in a forty-eight second time period they only read out one-fifth of the frame.

JB: Does that mean that basically they get a section of the image or, in a sense, that it reads every other line or something like that?

DL: There are a variety of software-selectable choices on board. They can send every other pixel of every other line; that cuts the data down by a factor of four. They can send seven-bit data instead of eight-bit; that cuts it down by one-eighth. They can send the middle fifty percent of the picture; they can send the first 480 lines, which is only sixty percent of the image. Those are all called edit modes, because they send the actual image data, but they don't send all of it. There are also data compression modes available

on board. In these the data goes through a processor, and it selects only, say, differences between pixels, or it looks at a region and says, "How many bits do I need to send back to get the majority of the information in this region?"

JB: So, for example, you are looking at a band on Saturn; to give you a sense of what that band is like, it will only really have to read part of the information, and it will come back faster.

DL: That's right. If the scene is relatively smooth, if it doesn't change much, it takes less bits to characterize it. This is something they have experimented with for over ten years, but I believe this is the first time they have implemented it on one of the planetary spacecraft.

JB: It's really fascinating that that becomes the way of getting information back as best as you can.

DL: But you give up some information.

JB: You give up some detail.

DL: That's the choice.

Encke Division in Saturn's outer A-ring seen from Voyager 2. This photograph was computer-generated from the spacecraft's photopolarimeter readings rather than from the vidicon camera. 8/25/81 (FC).

This wide-angle view was the last picture Voyager 2 took before crossing the ring plane. The F-ring is in the foreground, and several spokes appear as bright, horizontal streaks above the darker B-ring. 8/26/81 (B/W).

Saturn imaged in false colors from Voyager 1 (the so-called bumblebee photo) to increase the visibility of features in the north temperate belt. The photograph was taken through ultraviolet, green, and violet filters. 10/18/80 (FC).

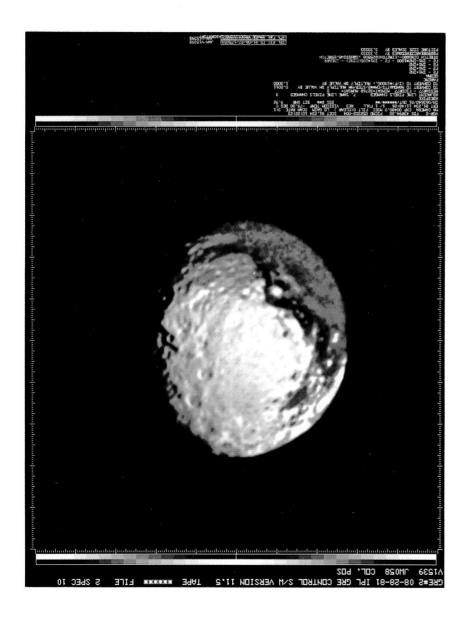

Saturn's moon Mimas (about 240 miles in diameter), as seen from Voyager 1, shows a large crater, Arthur, which is about eighty-one miles across. The central icy peak in the crater is over three miles high. 1980. (B/W).

Photograph from Voyager 2 of Saturn's moon Iapetus, the second-most remote Saturnian satellite. Iapetus, which revolves but does rotate, is unique in having a leading hemisphere less than one-tenth as bright as its trailing hemisphere. 8/22/81 (FC).

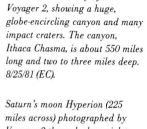

Saturn's moon Tethys, from Voyager 2, showing a huge, globe-encircling canyon and many impact craters. The canyon, Ithaca Chasma, is about 550 miles long and two to three miles deep. 8/25/81 (EC).

Saturn's moon Hyperion (225 miles across) photographed by Voyager 2 through clear, violet, and green filters. The irregular shape is probably the result of repeated impacts that have taken off large pieces. 8/24/81 (FC).

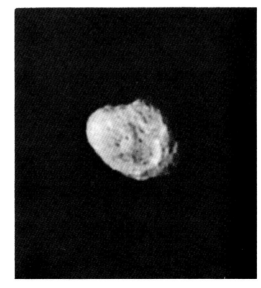

Saturn

DL: The individual experiment team members — there are atmosphere people, there are crater people, there are geologists — each of these experimenters has one or more different interests. They will look through the images that have been received — they can call them up and just electronically flip through them as you would a set of pictures — and select the ones that they want to do something special with. The next step usually involves personal interaction with the experimenter, when they discuss what they want to get out of the image or set of images. That is the key objective in this process, extracting and displaying information in a way that is most appropriate for interpretation by the scientists.

Photograph from Voyager 2 of Saturn's moon Enceladus taken from seventy-four thousand miles away through clear, violet, and green filters. In many ways, the surface of this satellite resembles that of Jupiter's moon Ganymede, but Enceladus in only one-tenth the latter's size. 8/25/81 (FC).

The same photograph of Enceladus from Voyager 2, the image strongly contrast-stretched to bring out surface detail. An extensive canyon and rectilinear fault lines can be seen. 8/25/81 (EC).

Saturn

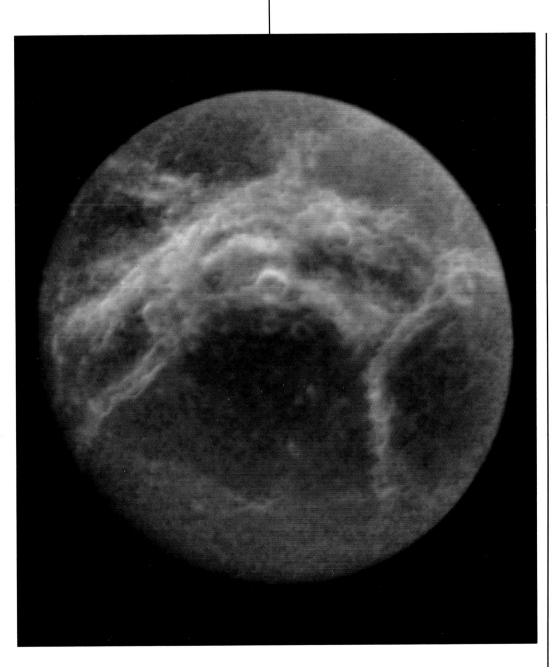

Image from Voyager 1 of large impact craters on Dione. Also visible are bright, radiating patterns, presumably surface deposits. 11/12/80 (B/W).

Image from Voyager 1 of large, bright streaks on the face of Dione taken from 417,000 miles away. Some of these streaks are grooves that may be the result of fracturing in the moon's surface. 11/12/80 (EC).

Voyager 1 details of the atmosphere covering Titan, taken from 13,700 miles away. Several high-altitude haze layers (in blue) are visible above the opaque red clouds, which completely cover the moon. 11/12/80 (FC).

JB: In terms of color, does that come back as an instantaneous image, or do you have to get three images?

DL: The latter. The Voyager cameras are monocolor, but they each have a filter wheel with eight positions, some clear and I think one duplicate.

JB: Just in case one of them . . .

DL: They may have duplicated some of the filter positions because they can only step through the wheel in one direction, and there are preferred directions such as "clear." They don't quite have a red. The cameras aren't sensitive to red; the filters are almost-red, green, blue, violet, ultraviolet, sodium and methane.

JB: What are sodium and methane?

DL: There are narrow bands in which methane and sodium emit, and there are narrow band filters that block out everything outside of that particular band.

JB: So those were specifically designed for Voyager, I take it.

DL: Specifically because they knew there was methane and sodium emission out there.

JB: So then the color is tricky. If you're circling, you have to go by three times to get three images or be in a situation where the computer will alter your angle to put it back into position.

DL: In fact, the latter is what is usually done. Three pictures are taken in sequence, and then we have to go in and register them. This is all done by the analyst who does the processing. Also you can't take the numbers just as they come out of the camera because the camera sensitivity through the different filters is different, so the images that are received have to be adjusted to compensate for these differences. This is done using data that was obtained when the cameras were calibrated on the ground. Years and years ago — this was back in '75, '76 — we calibrated the cameras on the ground through all the filter positions. In this calibration, the cameras were

exposed to uniform illumination fields which were accurately measured. The camera output was recorded at various levels along with the exposure time and illumination level. From these you can calculate basically what the sensitivity is at every picture element on the tube.

JB: Then what?

DL: You build up a set of calibration files that say, "For this output in this filter position, and at this exposure time, this was the irradiance at the aperture of the camera." Also, when you get the images back, you have to do a geometric correction to get the correct spatial representation of the scene; that is, you have to put all the pixels back where they are supposed to be. These camera tubes are magnetically focused and deflected, and they change with the magnetic field. The magnetic field around Jupiter is very different from that of the Earth or other planets. These tubes have over a hundred little marks, little squares, that are etched on the face of the tube. The locations of these marks have been very accurately measured with a theodolite through the camera lens, so that we know exactly what their position is relative to each other.

JB: And if you get a different magnetic field, you can adjust so you will get the same relationship between the pixels.

DL: Back to where we know what the geometry of the image was when it was received at the face of the tube.

JB: Amazingly complex.

DL: Now you go through and take each pixel in a given image and, given the output data value of that pixel, correct that value to represent the equivalent scene radiance at that pixel. From there you can reconstruct real color if you want.

JB: Or even real black and white.

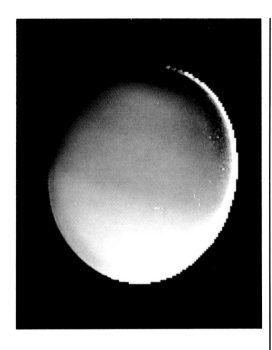

Photomosaic of Saturn's largest moon, Titan, from Voyager 1. Titan is the only satellite in the solar system known to have a substantial atmosphere. Special computer processing shows a pronounced difference in brightness between the northern and southern hemispheres. 1980 (EC).

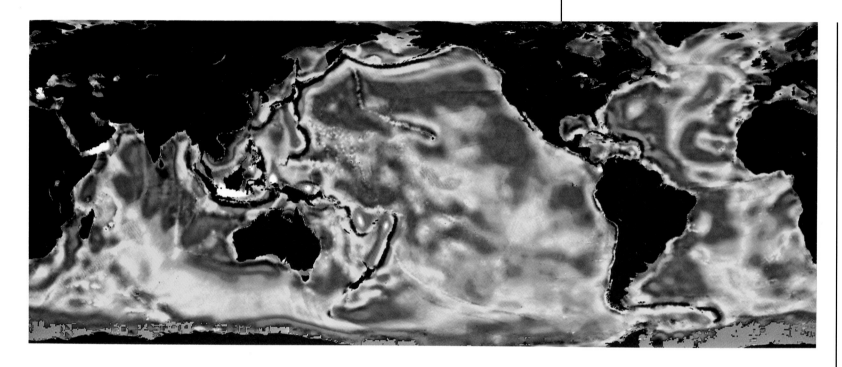

Topographic relief radar image from Seasat altimeter showing the elevations of the surfaces of the oceans. By measuring the ocean surface, the characteristics of the ocean floor become apparent. 7/7-10/10/78 (FC).

JB: Basically JPL got into the business of doing unmanned planetary probes. How did Seasat happen? How did JPL get involved in that particular project?

AH: There were some guys here working on radar, and one systems engineer pushed very hard for that whole project. Pushed it here and at NASA headquarters. Finally he transferred from here to NASA headquarters to really get the thing going. Now he is in business as a consultant. But I think the origin of this project at JPL was due to his saying that there are certain things you can look at in the ocean that require a different kind of equipment. Radar technique would be important, and he pushed very heavily for that; one reason JPL got it is because all his contacts with people who could design the radar equipment were here.

•

JB: The major part of Seasat was radar. That was all that was on board?

AH: No, there were passive microwave sensors, sensors that just measured the radiation coming from the Earth. It is a temperature sensor device.

JB: But in terms of image making . . .

AH: It was all radar. The imager was a synthetic aperture radar designed to observe the surface of the oceans.

•

JB: The information was gathered; Seasat died earlier than was expected. It was alive for one-hundred-plus days, something like that, and then somehow the information was not processed for a while, it was kind of let be. It just struck me as something interesting. You get a big Christmas present, and when you open it up you set it aside and forget about it.

AH: No, it wasn't ignored. The processing of the images is not easy. And there was some time just spent developing better and better techniques; it was cumbersome when we first started out.

JB: Maybe we had better go into that a little bit, the radar.

AH: Enormous amounts of data come back from the radar image, and the data has to go through a computer before it comes out as a picture. The radar does not send back a picture.

JB: The radar sends back information about the power generated by each of those patterns.

AH: Or by the complete pattern.

JB: And then it gets translated back into what the picture is that would have transmitted that amount of power.

AH: That power pattern.

JB: Do you feel that that winds up getting an image of what's out there as precise as the normal situation that you had with the vidicon?

AH: It's strange, because with the vidicon, the light comes in from the Sun, so everything is nice and shadowed the way your eyes see it. With the radar the light is coming from the instrument itself rather than from the Sun. Furthermore, the radar pays attention to how long it takes the beam to get there and go back again; that's fundamental to radar. And that helps to disentangle what part of the picture you are looking at when you do this mathematically. It gives some strange illusions over rough terrain. Valleys between mountains seem as far away as the mountain tops. It looks like the mountains are tilted toward you. But, of course, Seasat was designed to look at oceans, not mountains.

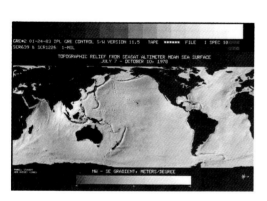

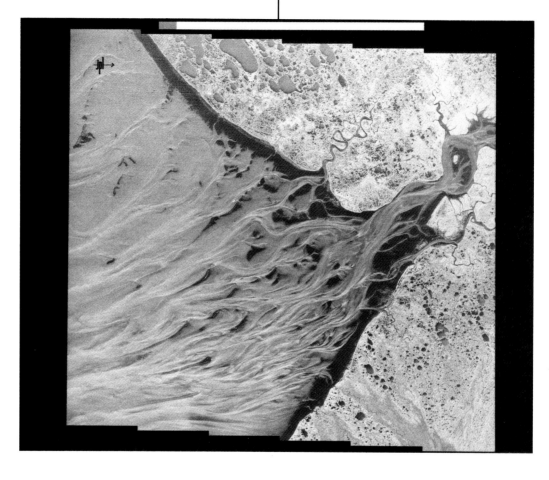

Topographic relief radar image from Seasat altimeter showing the elevations of the surfaces of the oceans. As can be seen in this image, Seasat has shown that the ocean is higher over seamounts or ridges and lower over trenches. 7/7-10/10/78 (FC).

Seasat radar image of the mouth of the Kuskokwim River, Alaska, which empties into the Bering Sea. Shallow-water bathymetry patterns are visible. 7/13/78 (B/W).

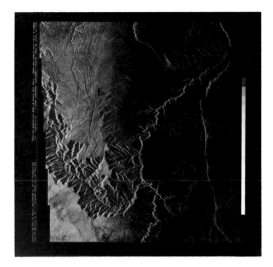

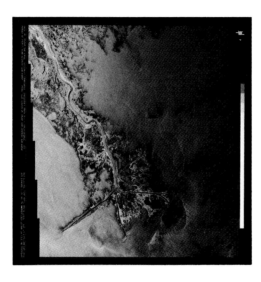

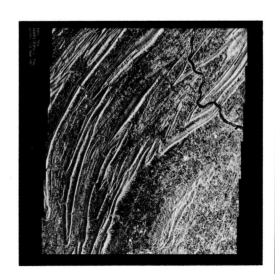

Seasat radar image of the Grand Canyon. 8/19/78 (B/W).

Seasat radar image of the Mississippi River delta. 7/24/78 (B/W).

Seasat radar image of the Allegheny Mountains near Harrisburg, Pennsylvania. The river is the Susquehanna. 8/78 (B/W).

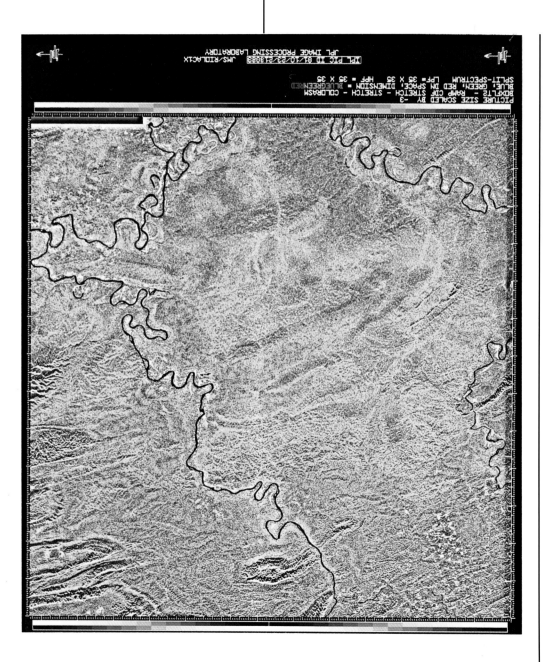

Color-classified Seasat image of a marginal ice zone in the Arctic Ocean off Banks Island. The colors denote different types of ice; blue is used for the ocean. 10/4/78 (FC).

Southern Mexico and Guatemala radar-imaged by Seasat. The imaging radar looks through the forest to the ground below, and special processing enhances geological details. 1978 (FC).

JB: The radar data comes back for Seasat, and also for SIR-A and SIR-B, and is basically made into black and white images. Why do they decide on occasion to make color images?

CL: In some cases, people find it easier to discriminate between the different sorts of materials if they are displayed in different colors.

JB: Rather than looking at a black and white image, however detailed such an image might be, and they are often quite detailed.

CL: Yes, they are, and in fact with this type of color — false color or pseudocolor — there is not really any more information contained in the color image than in the black-and-white image, but some people find it easier to see things.

•

JB: How is the decision made to use specific colors?

CL: That is very much a work of art, and each individual image is approached separately. The contents of the image are considered, and an attempt is made to try to distinguish different features. A color arrangement that will work for one image may or may not work for another image of a similar area or even an adjacent area.

•

JB: It's very peculiar for someone who doesn't know anything about this process to see an area that shows a tropical climate in these intense, almost Hawaiian shirt, shades or an area that shows a northern climate where things are, shall we say, evergreen green and more subdued. Do you attempt to use green for areas of vegetation, blue for the sea, or anything like that?

CL: In general, we picked blue for the ocean, but beyond that there was no conscious effort to correlate any sort of preconceived notion concerning color with what was there. Our main objective was to be able to display differently things which appeared differently to us.

JB: Seasat made two major discoveries. First, it determined that the height of the ocean parallels the height of the ocean floor, and second, it discovered what would one call them, megawave patterns?

AH: The subsurface waves.

JB: There is a wonderful shot of the Cape of Good Hope with these incredible waves coming out, and I guess even around Jamaica there is almost something like eddies of some sort.

AH: Also off of Nantucket, off of Baja California. There are waves coming out of the Columbia River. Why the radar saw those is still some matter of controversy.

JB: But there is no doubt about the fact.

AH: Oh, they match all the theoretical concepts about subsurface waves.

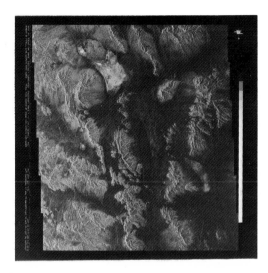

The area near Cadiz Lake, California, radar-imaged by Seasat. 8/13/78 (B/W).

Seasat view of internal waves in the Gulf of California. The tip of an island is visible at the bottom. The occurrence of these waves is associated with the twice-monthly cycle of spring tides. 9/17/78 (B/W).

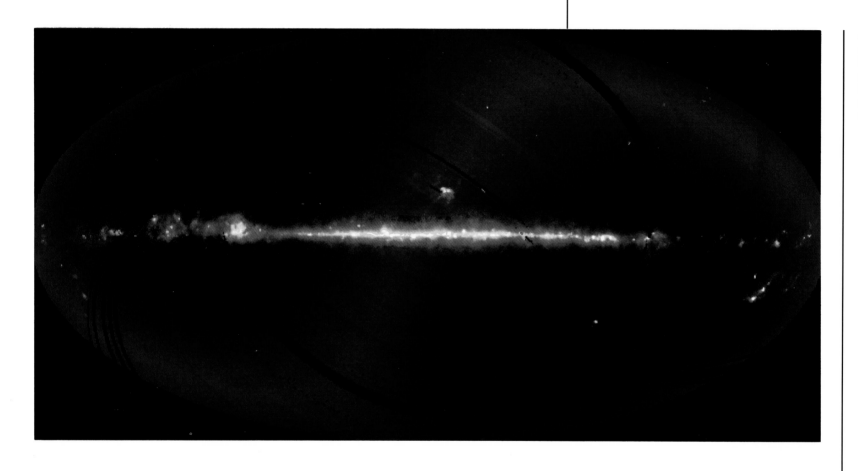

A view from IRAS of nearly the entire heavens. Our galaxy is the bright horizontal band with its center at the center of the picture. Hotter material appears blue or white, while cooler material is shown in red. 1983 (FC).

JB: IRAS doesn't seem to be a logical part of what JPL would do.

AH: No. We were getting more and more into the land-observing business.

JB: Which, for economic reasons, I would imagine, Washington might approve more easily.

AH: There's some concern about that.

JB: About the land stuff?

AH: About the economic justification. Because there is some feeling that history shows that as soon as you say, "This is an operational system, this has a practical application," the government will say, "Turn it over to the Department of Commerce." Like Landsat, for example; it is now run by the Department of Commerce, not by NASA — also weather satellites. So we hesitate to mention practical applications anymore, operating systems. We speak in terms of a research system for science — understand the Earth for scientific purposes; eventually people will evolve practical applications out of it, but NASA's job is to build these systems to get a scientific understanding. The objective is a global habitability program that is sometimes called NASA's Earth Sciences Program. Earth science from space. The reason that they have something called the Earth Observing System — that's a huge platform . . . well, now it is becoming smaller as the price estimates come in — is to make a scientific study of the Earth on a global basis, that's the statement here.

●

JB: In terms of IRAS, what were the decisions made about what it was going to look at?

AH: It was a survey, a complete sky survey.

JB: The whole thing?

AH: Oh, yes, so it was a constant routine of observations.

JB: I think of the Lunar Orbiter, except you're doing . . .

AH: The pattern was carefully worked out to complete this survey. You can't let the Sun shine in the lens, you can't let the Earth shine in the lens, and you only point it toward a certain piece of the sky. You very carefully strategize as to when you are going to look at which area of the sky and get it all done before the helium boils away.

JB: And did they do it?

AH: You can see the celestial map.

View from IRAS of nearly the entire heavens. The three-color composite has been stretched to reveal the S-shaped curve of faint heat emitted by dust in the plane of the solar system. 1983 (FC).

Ecliptic, cylindrical projection of nearly the entire heavens, viewed by IRAS. The S-shaped curve again shows the heat emitted by dust in the plane of the solar system. 1983 (FC).

Photomosaic from IRAS of the heart of our galaxy. The center of the picture is the center of the galaxy, while the yellow and green knots indicate giant clouds of interstellar gas. The warmest material is represented in blue, while colder material is shown in red. 1983 (FC).

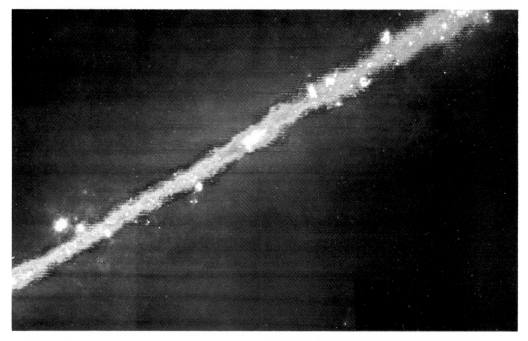

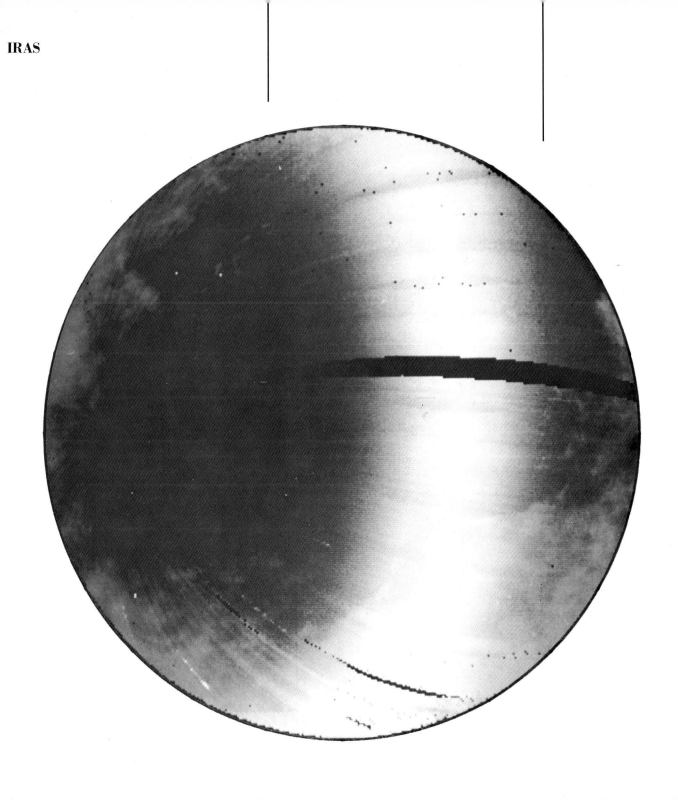

Unfiltered photographic map from IRAS of the area fifteen degrees around the north galactic pole. 1983 (FC).

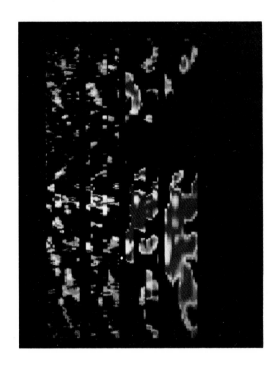

JB: IRAS was receiving light, not generating its own signal like radar.

AH: It was getting infrared.

JB: Basically IRAS is picking up created energy or heat rather than visible light per se.

AH: That's correct. It's getting what is called the thermal infrared.

JB: What do those images in IRAS really show you when you look at them?

AH: Well, first of all you can see clouds that aren't radiating visible light; they are too cold or they are too far away. The only way you can see clouds with a regular telescope is if there is a star nearby which reflects light off the cloud.

JB: But if it's far away from stars, it's going to be totally dark, of course.

AH: So this way we could see clouds that have no other illumination except from their own temperature, and their heat is radiating infrared to us, and you can see hot clouds behind cold clouds and that sort of thing. We could see clouds that very much corresponded to the theoretical prediction of what the formation of a star should be like. It should have a rather warm cloud of dust embedded in a cooler cloud; we saw several of these, and we saw them in areas where we are pretty sure star formation is going on because of some of the other characteristics.

JB: And the satellite is the first that really has done that, I mean that has really validated that theoretical prediction?

AH: We have quite a bit of stuff from high mountain observatories and more coming in, because we are getting better and better equipment, but they are still under some atmosphere; they are still at least ten times less sensitive.

●

JB: How long has the infrared been operative as a device for astronomical observations? Not very long, I guess.

AH: Thermal infrared required a very high altitude, and the kind of sensor technology for that type of infrared hasn't been around for long. It required cooling the thing down; you have to, otherwise it would be like taking a picture from inside a light bulb.

JB: So really there hasn't been that much before IRAS in terms of astronomical imaging.

IRAS scan across the Large Magellanic Cloud with four separate wavelength bands showing different levels of infrared measurements. The Large Magellanic Cloud is the closest galaxy to ours. 2/83 (FC).

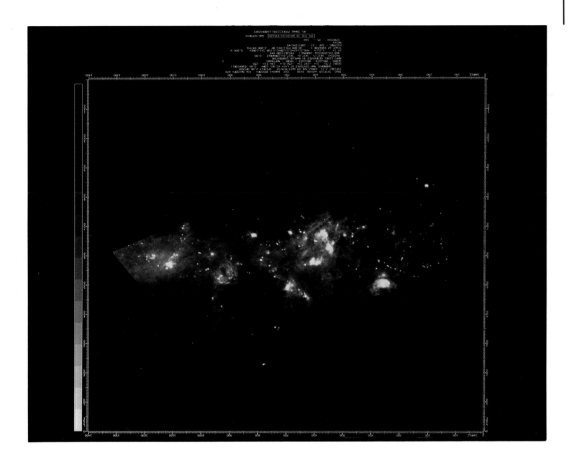

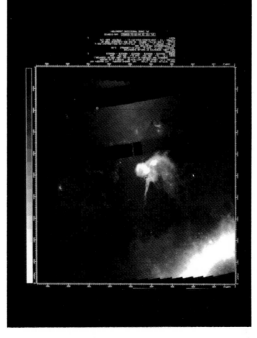

Photograph of a site of star formation from IRAS. 1983. (FC).

Photograph from IRAS of Scorpius-Ophiuchus cloud of interstellar gas and the galactic plane in yellow and red. 1983 (FC).

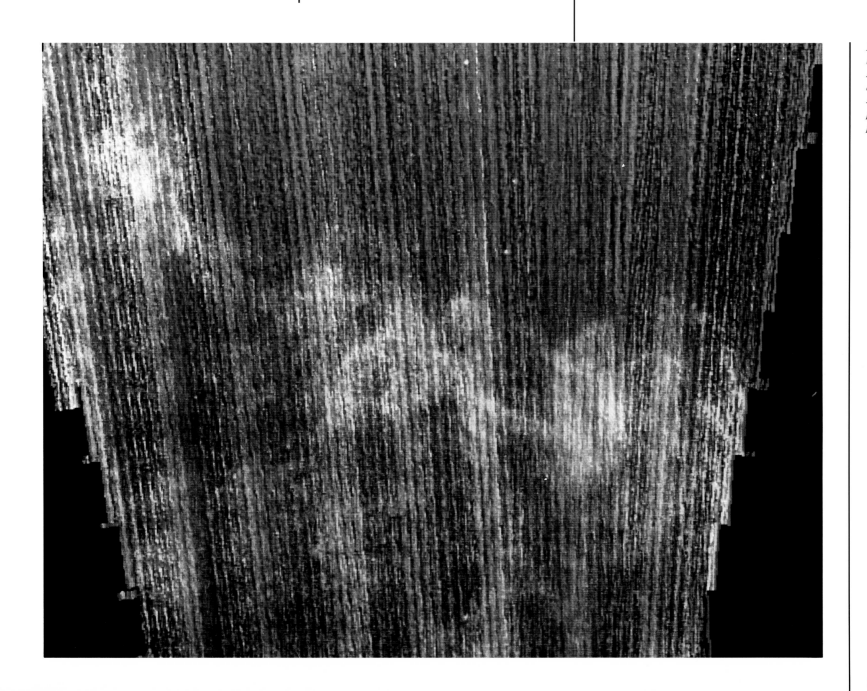

Photograph from IRAS of infrared cirrus clouds, the wispy structure extending horizontally across the image. The vertical strips are artifacts of the processing procedure and are not present in the sky. 1983 (FC).

JB: Looking at one of the IRAS images — for example, there is really an aesthetically beautiful one of the Milky Way — what happens then is that it is coded in arbitrarily to read blue where there is some heat and then red up to yellow where there is the most intense heat.

AH: As if you could shift your eyeballs down to that portion of the spectrum, although in fact that is the wrong way, because in the visible light range that you see blues are from the hottest sources, reds from the coldest sources.

JB: There is still a heck of a lot of data too.

AH: That is being processed. We're arguing, as you know, with the neighbors [in Pasadena] about building a special computing facility just for IRAS, a facility which will be working for years.

JB: Just to process the information because that satellite is no longer functioning.

This radar image of playas in northern Algeria was produced by digitally correlating data from SIR-A and Seasat. Digital combination of data greatly increases the potential for geologic mapping. 1982 (FC).

JB: Is there a situation on some of the images that are created on SIR-A and SIR-B where, beyond just mosaics, the same terrain is shot more than once to create the final image that you see?

CL: What's interesting about the survey instrument is that the antenna can be pointed in different directions relative to the Earth's surface. So if several passes are made over the same area, it's possible to coregister these images and have two or more different views of the same area. You can create a stereo effect from these images and get a better idea of what exists on the surface, because you can consider the scattering of the surface at different angles. It gives you more of a chance of understanding what's down there.

JB: So in some of the final images from SIR-B, coregistration of different passes at different angles was used to create the final image. In a very different way this relates somewhat to the way in which color is created from Voyager, for example, where there are three consecutive photographs . . .

CL: It's similar to that.

●

JB: A specific image leads toward certain color decisions.

CL: Yes, it does. In one image of Hawaii there were two frames which we received, and we applied false color to both of them separately. For the first frame we came up with a color scheme which distinguished the lava and ash flows from the vegetated areas.

JB: Are the lava and ash flows what turned out to be red in the photograph?

CL: Yes. On the other side of the island in the other image there weren't any lava or ash flows, and the things that we wanted to highlight were different, so we came up with a different color scheme for that image. Mosaicking those two directly, already colored, would not produce anything that was reasonable. However, if the images are mosaicked first . . .

JB: Then you create colors for the mosaicked image.

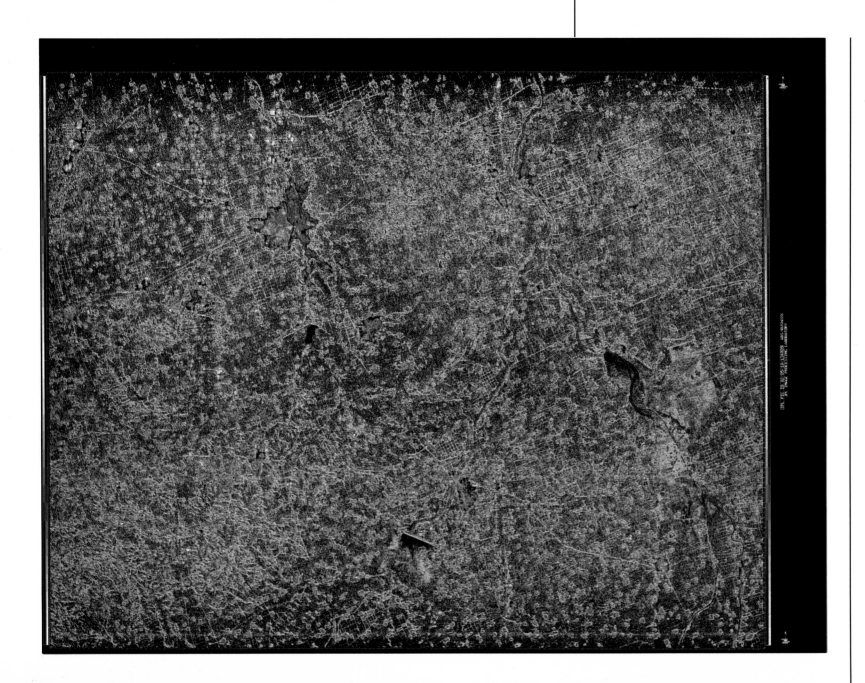

SIR-A radar image of Hopeh Province, People's Republic of China, showing patterns of villages (red spots) and wheat fields (green). The cities of An-chu and Wei-fang are visible at the center and center left in gray. 11/81 (FC).

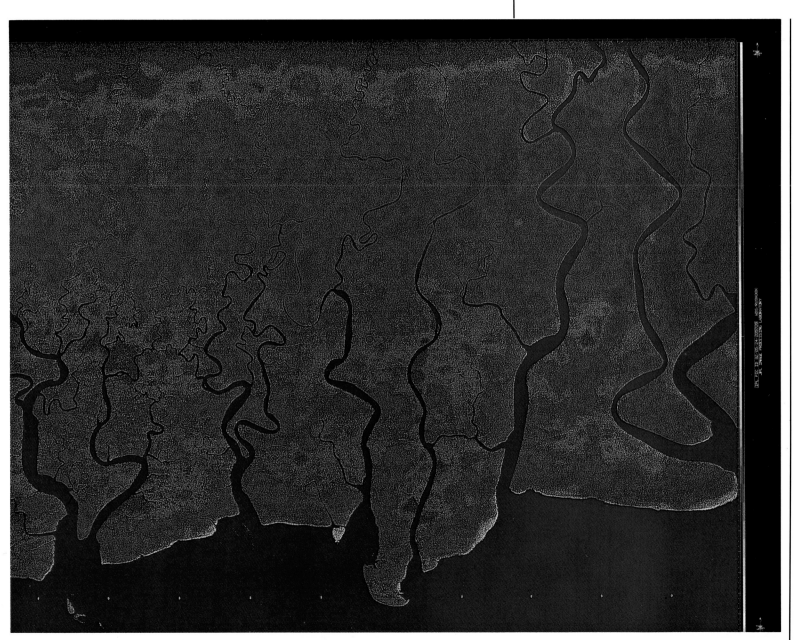

*SIR-A radar image of the swampy
south coast of New Guinea.
11/81 (FC).*

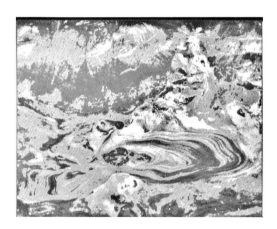

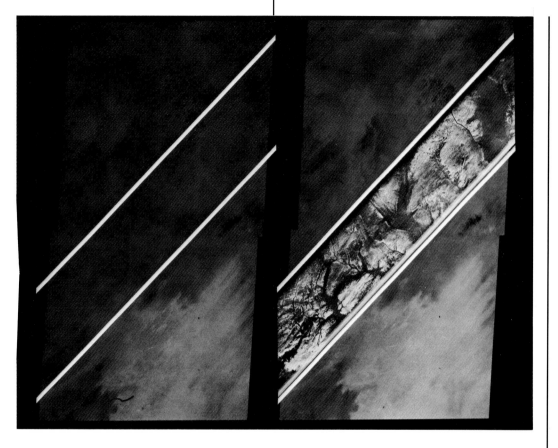

SIR-A radar image of the Great Salt Desert in Iran. The swirling patterns are outcroppings of Miocene and Pliocene sediments. 11/81 (FC).

Photograph from Landsat of part of the Sudanese desert. The same area is shown on the right with an inset of SIR-A radar imagery showing the pattern of former river systems that exists beneath the sand. Archaeological exploration at one of these former river sites resulted in the discovery of human artifacts. 11/81 (EC; B/W).

SIR-A radar image of the Kalpin Chol and Chong Korum mountains in Xinjiang Province, People's Republic of China. These mountains have been folded and faulted as the result of active tectonism and intense earthquakes. 11/81 (FC).

This SIR-A radar image shows a complicated strike-slip fault system (left to right) in north central China, an extension of a fault system over eighteen miles long. 11/81 (B/W).

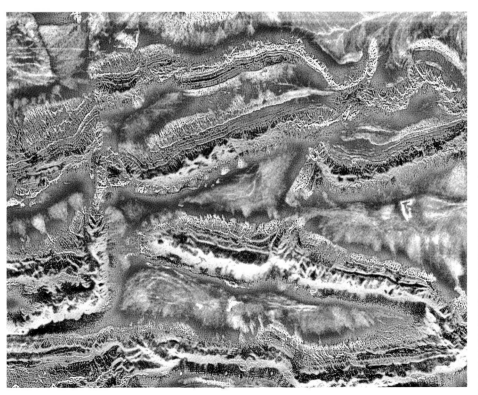

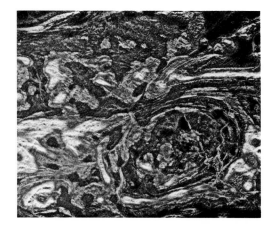

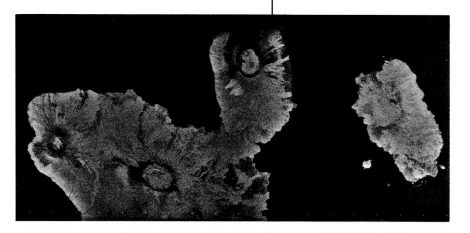

SIR-A radar image of part of the Hamersley Mountains in Western Australia. Red areas represent very rough mountain terrain; green ones represent desert-like areas; and blue ones represent smooth areas, such as dry lakebeds. 11/81 (FC).

SIR-A radar image of the western Galápagos Islands, Ecuador, showing volcanoes. Three of those volcanoes on Isabella Island (on the left) can be seen. 11/81 (B/W).

SIR-B radar image of the city of Montreal with the St. Lawrence River and Seaway to the right. Pink and blue areas generally represent buildings or pavement; green areas show regions of cultivation or natural vegetation. 10/7/84 (FC).

SIR-B radar image of the mouth of the Ganges River in Bangladesh during flood stage. 1984 (FC).

SIR-B radar image of folded, layered rocks of the Paleocene Age in the high plateau of northern Peru. The area shows extreme dissection and local offsets of rocks due to faulting. 10/7/84 (FC).

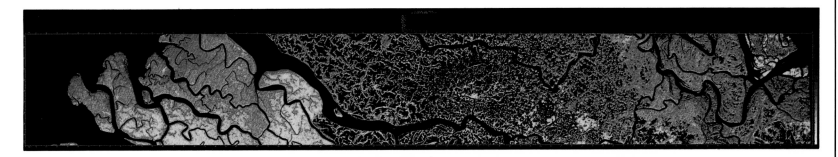

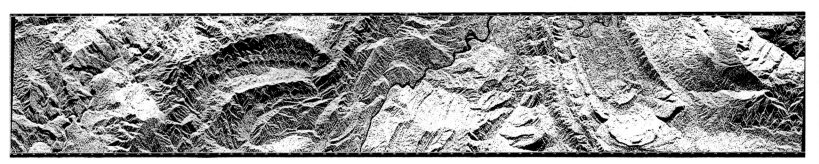

SIR-B radar mosaic photograph of the coast of the island of Hawaii. The red indicates smooth ash cover. Kilauea Crater is the circular feature in the center, and Hilo is on the bay on the right. 10/11/84 (FC).

AH: The big technology revolutions now are in computers and they are affecting the space race. You have to realize that even Galileo is nine- to ten-year-old technology. That's when the design was frozen, so what we could do now, starting over with a Galileo-like machine, would be a lot better.

JB: What is the date on Galileo?

AH: It will be launched next year.

JB: How long to get there?

AH: Two years, two and a half years. So by the time it gets to Jupiter in December of 1988, it will be thirteen-year-old technology in this day of technological change.

JB: Is that a bad result of that whole system that you were describing to me earlier where basically you have to sign off on everything?

AH: No, I don't think so. There is an engineering phrase, "the better is the enemy of the good," which is something to keep in mind.

JB: So it really is a trade-off situation.

AH: Picking the exact time to freeze the design. But you see, when we froze the design it was on the basis of the schedule we had been given on the availability of the shuttle flights, which was three years wrong. It should have been launched in 1983, or 1982, and that would have been much more reasonable. Taking advantage of the time, we do more testing, but on the original plan, we should have launched a couple of years ago.

•

JB: What exactly is Galileo going to be doing?

AH: As it approaches Jupiter, it will dispatch a probe to go into the edge of Jupiter's atmosphere; then it will deflect its own course so it won't go into the atmosphere. Instead it will fly by, and the probe then will go into the atmosphere and radio back.

JB: The probe will go in at an angle, not straight down, so there's as much time as you can get before . . .

AH: No, so it won't get burned up. As it goes in it gets very, very hot, and it has to spend longer time in the upper atmosphere to radiate some of that heat away before it gets down lower and plunges straight on in. Then the Galileo goes into orbit around Jupiter. It goes past the moons of Jupiter and uses the gravity of each moon to change its course a little bit and go on to the next one. It will keep doing this for a couple of years and go past all the major moons of Jupiter.

JB: With a lot of time spent at Io, I'm sure.

AH: Not too much. Io is in a heavy radiation region, and that damages electronics.

JB: The possibility for images is rather extraordinary.

AH: And we've got some good infrared spectrometers, so Galileo will be able to get good data on the geology and the actual chemical nature of the surfaces as well.

JB: This is not something that Voyager accomplished, is it?

AH: That's right. We had infrared but not this good. Voyager didn't spend much time near these moons, and didn't get anywhere near as close.

Mission Name	Objective	Launch Date	Encounter Date	No. of Photos Returned
Ranger 7	Acquire and transmit photographs of the lunar surface before impacting the Moon.	July 28, 1964	Impacted Moon *(Sea of Clouds)* July 31, 1964	4,316
Ranger 8	Same as above.	February 17, 1965	Impacted Moon *(Sea of Tranquility)* February 20, 1965	7,137
Ranger 9	Same as above.	March 21, 1965	Impacted Moon *(Alphonsus Crater)* March 24, 1965	5,814
Surveyor 1	Lunar soft landing. Provide data in support of the Apollo program.	May 31, 1966	*(Ocean of Storms)* June 1, 1966	11,240
Surveyor 3	Same as above.	April 16, 1967	*(Ocean of Storms)* April 19, 1967	6,326
Surveyor 5	Same as above.	September 8, 1967	*(Sea of Tranquility)* September 10, 1967	19,118
Surveyor 6	Same as above.	November 6, 1967	*(Sinus Medii)* November 9, 1967	29,952
Surveyor 7	Lunar soft landing. Scientific exploration of a lunar highland region. Provide data in support of the Apollo program.	January 6, 1968	*(near Tycho crater)* January 9, 1968	21,038
Lunar Orbiter 1*	Photographic mapping program of lunar equatorial region (43°E to 50°W) to aid in the selection of suitable landing sites for Surveyor and Apollo.	August 10, 1966	Impacted Moon October 29, 1966	207
Lunar Orbiter 2	Same as above.	November 6, 1966	Impacted Moon October 11, 1967	211

Mission Name	Objective	Launch Date	Encounter Date	No. of Photos Returned
Lunar Orbiter 3	Photograph twelve Apollo/Surveyor landing sites that were identified by screening Lunar Orbiter 1 and 2 photos. Provide gravitational field and lunar environment data.	February 4, 1967	Impacted Moon October 9, 1967	182
Lunar Orbiter 4	Photographic survey of lunar surface features for scientific purposes. Gravitational field, micrometeoroid, and radiation experiments.	May 4, 1967	Impacted Moon October 6, 1967	163
Lunar Orbiter 5	Photograph five potential Apollo landing sites previously viewed by Lunar Orbiters 1, 2, and 3, as well as several locations for Surveyor landings. Monitor proton radiation and meteoroids in vicinity of Moon.	August 1, 1967	Impacted Moon January 31, 1968	212
Mariner 4	Mars flyby. Perform scientific measurements in interplanetary space between the orbits of Earth and Mars, and in the vicinity of Mars.	November 28, 1964	July 14, 1965	21
Mariner 6	Mars flyby over equator to study Martian surface and atmosphere.	February 24, 1969	March 27, 1969	75
Mariner 7	Mars flyby over southern hemisphere.	March 27, 1969	August 4, 1969	126
Mariner 9	Study of Mars from orbit. Map the planet and look for sites for Viking landers. Mariner 9 took first pictures showing surface of Mars' two moons, Deimos and Phobos.	May 30, 1971	November 13, 1971	7,329

Mission Name	Objective	Launch Date	Encounter Date	No. of Photos Returned
Mariner 10	Flyby of Venus and Mercury. First spacecraft to use the gravity of one planet (Venus) to reach another.	November 3, 1973	Venus: February 5, 1974; Mercury: March 29, 1974; Mercury: September 21, 1974; Mercury: March 16, 1975	November 1973: 1,000 (Earth/Moon); February 1974: 3,500 (Venus); March/April 1974: 2,300 (Mercury); September 1974: 1,000 (Mercury II); March 1973: 400 (Mercury III)
Viking 1**	Study the planet Mars from orbit and surface. Land an instrumented spacecraft on the surface of Mars.	August 20, 1975	Orbit: June 19, 1976; landing: July 20, 1976, Chryse Planitia (22.4° N, 47.5° W)	More than 50,000 from both landers and orbiters of Viking 1 and 2.
Viking 2	Same as above.	September 9, 1975	Orbit: August 7, 1976; landing: September 3, 1976, Utopia Planitia (48° N; 226° W)	See above.
Voyager 1	Fly past and study Jupiter and five of its major satellites (Io, Europa, Ganymede, Callisto, and Amalthea); Saturn and four of its satellites (Titan, Tethys, Enceladus, and Rhea).	September 5, 1977	Jupiter, Io, Ganymede, Europa, and Amalthea, March 5, 1979. Callisto, March 6, 1979; Titan, November 11, 1980; Saturn, Tethys, Enceladus, and Rhea, November 12, 1980	More than 35,000 photos of Jupiter were returned by both Voyager 1 and 2, and more than 33,000 of Saturn.
Voyager 2	Fly past and study Jupiter and five of its major satellites (Io, Europa, Ganymede, Callisto, and Amalthea); Saturn and nine of its satellites (Iapetus, Hyperion, Titan, Dione, Mimas, Enceladus, Tethys, Rhea, Phoebe); and possibly continue to Uranus and Neptune.	August 20, 1977	Callisto, July 8, 1979; Jupiter, Io, Ganymede, Europa, and Amalthea, July 9, 1979. Iapetus, August 22, 1981; Hyperion, August 24, 1981; Saturn, Titan, Dione, Mimas, Enceladus, Tethys, and Rhea, August 25, 1981; Phoebe, September 4, 1981	See above.

Mission Name	Objective	Launch Date	Encounter Date	No. of Photos Returned
Seasat	"Proof-of-concept" mission. Study world's oceans from near-polar orbit, 500 miles high. Provide scientific data for oceanographers, meteorologists, and commercial users of the seas. Carry instruments to measure ocean currents, tides, waves, surface temperatures, cloud patterns, and ice fields.	June 26, 1978		40 hours of data recorded covering approximately 96,000,000 square kilometers.
IRAS	Polar orbit satellite to chart the universe using extreme low temperature detectors to measure infrared energy, or heat emissions, from dust, gas, stars, galaxies, and other objects not observable through previously used optical detectors.	January 25, 1983		More than 200,000.
SIR-A	Observe the Earth by use of radar imagery; acquire and transmit data of different geologic regions; demonstrate the capability of the Space Shuttle as a platform for making spaceborne scientific investigations.	November 12, 1981		8 hours of data recorded covering approximately 10,000,000 square kilometers.
SIR-B	Same as above, but with a variable antenna to allow different observation angles to acquire multiple radar images.	October 5, 1984		16 hours of data recorded covering approximately 15,000,000 square kilometers of ocean and land.

*All Luner Orbiter missions managed by Langley Research Center, Hampton, Virginia, in cooperation with JPL.

**Viking 1 and 2 managed by Langley Research Center throughout development, launch, primary and extended mission. Managed by JPL as of April 1, 1978, for continued mission operations.

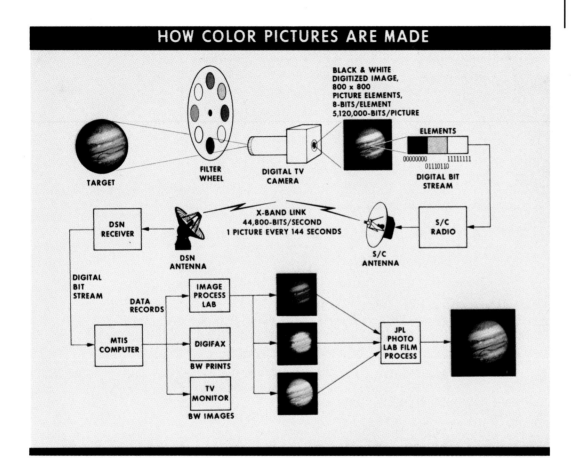

HOW COLOR PICTURES ARE MADE

BLACK & WHITE
DIGITIZED IMAGE,
800 x 800
PICTURE ELEMENTS,
8-BITS/ELEMENT
5,120,000-BITS/PICTURE

ELEMENTS

00000000 11111111
01110110

DIGITAL BIT
STREAM

TARGET

FILTER
WHEEL

DIGITAL TV
CAMERA

X-BAND LINK
44,800-BITS/SECOND
1 PICTURE EVERY 144 SECONDS

DSN
RECEIVER

DSN
ANTENNA

S/C
RADIO

S/C
ANTENNA

DIGITAL
BIT
STREAM

DATA
RECORDS

IMAGE
PROCESS
LAB

MTIS
COMPUTER

DIGIFAX

BW PRINTS

TV
MONITOR

BW IMAGES

JPL
PHOTO
LAB FILM
PROCESS

DL: In this case there is a "black and white camera" sitting out there. It is taking pictures at different times, and these pictures must go through a whole set of processes to transform the images to produce the best estimate of what the scene really looks like. Then, a person may sit down and adjust the color and the brightness until he or she gets what is aesthetically pleasing. Two people may produce — given the same data — different-looking pictures. One is pleasing and one is not; that's the art, the choice of what parameters you adjust.

JB: You talked to me about the fact that there are some people who are really capable of creating a photograph that is both pleasing and functions as it needs to, and there are some people who can't do that as well.

DL: That's right. And the choice of what processes to use and what programs to subject the picture to is more of an art in a sense than a science because so much depends upon what is in the data and what you want to get out of it. And it's very hard to write a complete prescription for that in advance.

•

DL: You start out with an image from the spacecraft, a digital image. In the processing, things like the camera response and the geometric distortion are all taken out. Then you may do an enhancement to create a more easily interpretable image, and you do what we call masking: you run the image through a program which adds all this annotation and organizes the image so that when you do create the negative or the film product, all of this good information is annotated on it. You can go back later — and the intent is always to be able to go back later — and identify what was done to that image, where it came from, when and how was it produced.

JB: And this happens at the Image Processing Laboratory.

DL: The GRE [ground reconstruction equipment]

was part of the Image Processing Laboratory at the time this picture was made. The creation of photoproducts is a two-step process; first you create the digital image with all of the annotation added, but it is still digital and on tape. That tape is taken over to another device (in this case the GRE) which does the digital-to-film conversion.

JB: On this image of Deimos (*fig. a*), for example, what does the printed information on the photograph mean?

DL: Starting with the *IPL PIC ID*, that's a unique number that was put on when the picture was processed in the computer with all of the attendant information. That number identifies the image. *DAE* are initials identifying who did the processing, and the number *12578* records the request submitted to the IPL to produce this image or set of images.

JB: Does the *AX* mean anything in particular?

DL: The *X* only had significance to the computer. The *I* preceding the request number indicates that this was a Viking Orbiter project request, and the *A* may be a version number; in cases where you have a number of jobs within the same request, you might label those A, B, C, D.

JB: What about the information above?

DL: This particular image was generated on the GRE film recorder. The annotation at the top gives information regarding when and how the GRE created the negative. Since this image was originally on tape, you could have a number of different negatives produced from the digital image; they could be created in a variety of ways. The *IPL PIC ID* refers to when the digital picture was created; the *GRE* data explains how the photographic negative was created, so you could go back and reproduce it if you wanted to. These gray scales adjacent to the image are put on when the digital image is created; they allow you to see whether the print or negative has as wide a dynamic range as possible, or to see whether the image is printed too dark or too light. The

IPL PIC ID 78/05/05/023226
JPL IMAGE PROCESSING LABORATORY
DAE/I2578AX

Figure A.
Photograph from Viking Orbiter 1 of Deimos, which is seven-and-a-half miles in diameter and smaller than its counterpart, Phobos. 5/5/78 (EC).

gray scale at the top of the page is put on the GRE and allows you to calibrate or to control the step between the negative and print if you want.

JB: In terms of the scale around the image . . .

DL: Those are called tic marks, and they indicate the number of picture elements, or pixels. Each small tic mark is five lines or five pixels, each larger one is twenty-five.

JB: So this basically measures the amount of information that you had available to make that image.

DL: Yes. In some cases where you have a rather small image, you don't have that many pixels.

JB: What about the information below?

DL: The annotation below the tic marks describes the project; *VO75* is Viking Orbiter. There is a picture number somewhere, a unique ID number. On this other photo, of Jupiter (*fig. b*) taken by Voyager 1, some of this is easier to read. *FDS* is a number generated by the flight data system, a clock on the spacecraft; it provides unique identification of when the picture was taken. The

PICNO is generated by the people on the ground, since the FDS is just a clock and pictures aren't taken all the time. These sequential picture numbers are generated on the ground so that we can tell when pictures are missing.

JB: Again, this is a unique number that is identified with a specific image.

DL: Yes. *SCET* is Spacecraft Event Time in GMT, or Greenwich Meridian Time. It tells when the picture was taken. The time the picture was taken is totally different from the time when the picture reaches the ground. *NAC* stands for narrow angle camera; *EXP* is the exposure time, and *MSEC* indicates that the value is in milliseconds; *FILT* indicates the filter through which the picture was taken. There is an eight-position filter on the camera. This is filter position one, which for the camera passes violet light. In the camera electronics, there is a low and high gain state. This image was taken in the low gain state. The scan range is one to one; these are slow scan cameras, and you have the capability of reading out a full frame in forty-eight seconds — that's one to one — or reading it out in three frame times — that would be a three-to-one slow scan; it would take, let's see, two and four-tenths minutes to read out a picture at a three-to-one scan rate. Thus the spacecraft reads a third of it out in the first forty-eight seconds, and a third of it in the next forty-eight seconds. The Voyagers also have five-to-one slow scan or ten-to-one slow scan rates. *ERT* is earth received time. This is a time tag that's put into the collected telemetry when it is received at the deep space station. Again, you can have the same picture come down different several times if it was recorded on the spacecraft tape recorder.

JB: And is the station actually JPL?

DL: No, it's Goldstone, in the Mojave Desert, or outside of Madrid, Spain, or in Australia. What else do we have? Full resolution is what *FULL RES* means, because there are edit modes on the spacecraft where we can send down partial pictures. *Vidicon temp* is the temperature of the face of the vidicon at the times the picture was taken, because the calibration, the sensitivity, of the vidicon is a function of temperature. Then let's see, *IN* and *OUT,* I think those are basically tape numbers. *DSS* is deep space station number; it isn't on here. *BIT SNR* is the signal ratio, an average bit signal-to-noise ratio during the time this picture was received. *Adjacent line pixels* refers to one of the processes that the pictures are put through on the ground here in the Image Processing Lab. If you had a very noisy picture, you would have a lot of "salt and pepper" all over the image. The *DESPIKE* algorithm goes through and looks for individual pixels that deviate too much from their neighbors; that indicates the particular pixel is probably in error. The algorithm then attempts to correct that error. *FICOR* stands for full intensity correction. It involves looking at each pixel and going to the calibration tables to see what the input light

intensity at that pixel would have been to give the output value that has been recorded.

JB: This has to do with all the calibrations you've done on the ground where, for example, you have your color wheel and you determine what that would do under certain conditions before you send the camera up in space.

DL: Exactly.

JB: And then you can do the correction because that obviously is not the raw image that you are going to get back.

DL: *FICOR 77* indicates that a full intensity correction was done on this image; every pixel was looked up in the radiometric calibration tables. Because vidicons are basically magnetically controlled there is a lot of geometric distortion in a vidicon image. In order to enable us to take that distortion out, little squares are etched on the face of the vidicon tube. They make up the dot pattern you see.

JB: What is the dot pattern that I see in the images again and again?

DL: On the ground, geometric calibration is also part of the calibration process; a theodolyte is used to measure the coordinates of each of those little squares; they are called reseaux. The pattern is called a reseau pattern. The center or the location of each of those is very accurately measured. There is a program called *RESSAR 77*; it's on the photo of Jupiter. It goes in and uses a very complicated program and basically finds the center location of each reseau. This program actually can locate that center to within a tenth of a pixel.

JB: So it can compensate, if a distortion occurs.

DL: In effect the program says, "Here is where those things are in the picture and here's where they should be to be geometrically correct. Now create a set of geometrical distortion parameters that will put the pixels back where they should be to correctly represent the scene." That's what *GEOMA* does; *GEOMA* is the geometric

Figure B.
As it moved rapidly away from Jupiter, Voyager 1 looked at the planet's lighted crescent. The Great Red Spot is visible below the equator. 4/4/79 (EC).

correction program that takes the coordinates that came out of *RESSAR* and does all of the calculations required to shift the pixels around to put them in the right geometric relationships.

JB: The whole issue is to see the image the way it really was, rather than how it was distorted by the tube.

DL: Yes, exactly. In fact *RESSAR* then goes in and does a little averaging so you don't see the little squares any more.

JB: Except that sometimes you do . . .

DL: Well, that's because they didn't run a *RESSAR* removal program. You can run *RESSAR* without doing the reseaux removal.

JB: What else haven't we done here yet?

DL: OK. *F2* is a program to do arithmetic operations using more than one picture. In this photo of Jupiter, most likely it was used either because they were going to do color and were doing something special, or possibly they were combining several different versions of this same image. The same image may have been sent back over several different data paths and they may have had to put them all together into one good image. *FARENC* stands for far encounter. Because we are producing color pictures using three images taken at different times, the position and size of the planet will be slightly different in each image; *FARENC* goes in and locates the limb of the planet [the edge of the planet] in the photograph, and reads the pixel location of each limb point. It fits an ellipsoid to these limb points and calculates the corresponding location of the center of the planet. Then the centers of the planet in the three images and the limbs are calculated. It's a way of doing registration between the three images.

JB: And what does *STRETCH* and *FILTER* refer to?

DL: Contrast enhancement. In this case the filter was probably an MTF filter, which sharpens up the image by compensating for the slight dispersion of each point by the camera — *MTF* stands for modulation transfer function. A point source imaged through the lens and onto the vidicon actually gets spread out. This process tightens it up as best we can, given our calibration data.

JB: In terms of making it more precise?

DL: And sharper. *COLORBALVL* is a program for taking the three images, combining them, and doing the appropriate intensity corrections and adjustments so that you get representative colors that still fit within the spectral capabilities of the photoproduct.

JB: So, given the three images that you need to do this, if there was a significant amount of variation you would want to somehow even it out.

DL: Yes. You might end up with the red so bright for some reason that it becomes saturated and this color is distorted; this program would look at all three colors, put them together, and do an intensity adjustment so that you don't saturate any more than you want. . . . . *SIZE* refers to magnification, either blowing the image up or reducing it. These are all individual programs that are used at the discretion of the analyst or the person who wants the picture processed.

JB: Let's go back to the image of Deimos again (*fig. a*). What are the graphs that appear at the bottom?

DL: These are histograms. They represent nine different steps in the process. A histogram represents the population of intensities in the image. This picture started out with an image that was really quite dark. Going across, this is the histogram of the initial blue image, the initial green, and the initial red. They are all relatively dark. In the left-hand column, the two lower rows show the before and after histograms of the hue of the picture. The color program that takes the three images and converts them to a different color space is called HSI for hue saturation and intensity. I think of Hue in terms of the "color" or location in spectrum from blue to red.

JB: So this basically points to a rather limited range of hue on this particular view.

DL: Now the two lower rows in the center column refers to the before and after histograms of the Saturation for that picture. Saturation is the degree of purity of the color.

JB: Is this a low or high degree of purity?

DL: Relatively low. So the color is muted. Intensity — represented in the lower rows of the right-hand column — is brightness.

JB: And this is very very dull; there's not a whole lot of light on that satellite at all.

DL: That's right; it doesn't reflect much, so the satellite appears gray. Using this *HSI* program you can do a stretch in color space, and you have the option of enhancing the Hue, the Saturation, or the Intensity, or you can manipulate all three.

JB: And they have done it all here.

DL: They put histograms on here because it's very easy to do a color stretch where you have saturated something and you don't know it. Especially if you work with the individual colors before you combine them. You can saturate something and never be aware of it, and you don't want to do that; one of the reasons you have all these nine histograms is so that you can evaluate the results of each step in the process and make sure you haven't done something you didn't want to do. From these histograms you can see what was done to the Hue; they've cut and narrowed down the Hue and the same with the Saturation. They've narrowed the spectrum and increased the purity of the color and then enhanced the Intensity. Given what Deimos is probably like, they would have squeezed the Hue because Deimos is probably a more or less monochromatic body. They would have squeezed the Saturation for the same reason, and had to expand the Intensity because Deimos reflects so little light.